Keys to Successful Living

by ALVIN H. GOESER
Director of Public Relations
World Insurance Company

Publishers
T. S. DENISON & CO., INC.
Minneapolis

Printed in the U. S. A.
By THE BRINGS PRESS

International Copyright Secured
Library of Congress Catalog Card Number 61-7835

To

Katharine Allan Goeser

with love

CONTENTS

7

11

PREFACE

The essays in this book were used as weekly and semi-monthly letters, and as pamphlets during the period from 1953 to date in the Public Relations program of the World Insurance Company of Omaha, Nebraska. Some were copyrighted by the company.

The World Insurance Company has consented to their use for assembling into book form under the title, *Keys to Successful Living*, reserving the right, however, to continue the use of the essays as in the past.

ALVIN H. GOESER
Director of Public Relations
World Insurance Company

BEING A SUCCESSFUL PERSON

We live in a culture in which success is measured largely by material accomplishments.

As a result of this we are preoccupied with things to accomplish and ends to reach. Our thoughts are of goals of action. We strive primarily to do. In our oral and written precepts the emphasis is on the importance of objectives and on methods of obtaining them or of reaching them.

Doing and accomplishing things, is, however, only half the story of successful living. Perhaps it is less than half. Action is important, but it is by no means the sole measuring stick of a successful life.

There is also such a thing as "being" as opposed to "acting." It is the person we are in contrast to the person in the pursuit of material objectives. It is ourselves as we are in terms of our peace of mind, our friendliness, our equanimity, our sense of justice, and our good will toward men.

As opposed to what we are striving to accomplish, "being" is what we are in terms of the inner relationships we have established with ourselves, with our fellow men, and with our destinies. It is what we are in terms of the values we live by and the conclusions we accept as to the meaning and purpose of our lives.

Gaining material objectives is important, but being a mature, well-balanced, wholesome person is not a tittle less so. Who will say, for instance, that gaining objectives such as

14

making a fortune is as great a feat as is living with peace in one's heart? Who will say that designing and manufacturing a new product for the convenience of man is of greater value than being a person whose friendliness, tolerance, and empathy make his presence a comfort to his fellow men? Or who will say that fame from one's deeds has the same priceless value as does the ability to smile with one's heart?

Without in any way minimizing the importance of material accomplishments, one must agree that the greater accomplishment is to be a person who is at peace with himself and whose wholesomeness diffuses peace, comfort, and good will to the men and women with whom he associates.

"To do" is one thing, but "to be" is another, and he who in the conquests of material objectives has neglected to be successful as a person will find his conquests illusory. Successful living requires both: "being" and "doing," but the greater is being a successful person. Doing will follow as a natural consequence.

THE THREE "MUSTS"

It is our belief that there are three simple "musts" underlying every successful endeavor.

These "musts" as we see them are:

1. Get a clear vision or picture of exactly what you want to do, or to accomplish in life.

2. Believe that you can and will succeed in doing it.

3. Start now to do it and keep at it.

*   *   *   *

Students of the failures and successes of human beings have long ago agreed that the first and greatest factor in success is a goal—a clear picture of exactly what an individual wants.

There must be a clearly defined objective—a specific goal to work towards—a bull's eye to shoot at. Know what you want and make a beeline for it.

The wanderer with no specific destination gets lost on the side roads.

*   *   *   *

Having set a goal, believe firmly, deeply, unflinchingly that you will attain it. Do not allow doubt to creep into your thinking. Cut it mercilessly out of your mind.

Believing is a habit. It can be developed by making yourself believe. Set about to form this habit of belief—belief in people, in life, in God; belief in yourself, in your innate greatness, in your ability to get that which you want most out of life.

You have your objective; you have built your dream castle in the clouds. You firmly believe that you will realize it. Now —get busy! Today—right now. Put the foundation under it! Make it come true.

Little by little; brick by brick; slowly, surely, patiently, confidently, unwaveringly! It is a long pull. But keep at it—hour by hour, day by day. Have faith! It is shaping!

Believe in yourself. Believe in the ultimate realization of your vision. Keep on working at it, and you will work a miracle as surely as day follows night.

*　*　*　*

Yes, these are the three simple but great wands of success:

1. A specific goal.

2. Belief in your ability to reach it.

3. Work—now, and keep at it.

THE MILL THAT RETURNS IN KIND

In his essay "On Philosophy and Friendship" Seneca, an immortal philosopher and writer of the first century of our Christian era, gives expression to one of the greatest of the principles of effective living.

Speaking of friendship he says, "If you ask how one can make a friend quickly, I will tell you." And then he quotes Hecato, another great philosopher, but of the century before Christ: "I can show you a philtre, compounded without drugs, herbs, or any witch's incantation: *'If you would be loved, love.'* "

It is as simple as all that. *"If you would be loved, love."* If you want the affection or devotion of your friends and associates, give it; if you want the loyalty or cooperation of your employees, give it; if you want good will from your customers and from the public, give good will to them. In a word, give to them what you would like to have them give to you.

This great principle, however, is not confined to friendship. It is one that is universally applicable to life. Re-stated in a slightly different way, it means that we can expect from life exactly that which we give to it. Life is a giant mill that feeds back to us exactly what we feed into it.

If we want understanding from it; if we want justice, charity, cooperation, or good will, we must first give it to life. It must come initially from us. Life pays off in kind. For love it returns love. For hostility it returns hostility. It cannot give back what is not given to it.

Success, well-being, and happiness are the end result of the processing by life of the ingredients we have fed into it. They are not accidental. They are not the results of special fortune or favor. They are merely the constituent wholes for which we have furnished the elemental substances.

We are naturally inclined to blame fortune or life when things are not shaping themselves well for us. This usually, however, is a form of self-compensation. It is an unconscious process of nature to help us retain our self-respect and self-worth. The real truth in most cases is that we are reaping the harvest of our own seeding and planting. We are getting back what we are daily giving.

Perhaps Hecato's simple principle is worth remembering in its universal application. "If you would be loved, love." Give what you wish to receive, and it will be given to you. Life is a giant mill that feeds back in kind.

A MARK OF MATURITY

To deal consistently with our fellow human beings with tact and dignity is one of the distinctive marks of personal maturity.

It takes emotional "grown-upness" to be considerate of the feelings of others and to show respect for the dignity that is inherent in the nature of all men, be they strong or weak, rich or poor, influential or unknown.

It is a mark by which we can unmistakably separate the boy from the man, the infant from the adult. Tact and considerateness, or what is the same thing, respect for the feelings and dignity of others is too difficult to be feigned and too genuinely real to be pretended. It is found only in him whose maturity has ripened into reverence for the human personality, and who by having equated all persons with himself gives to them the same reverence that he holds for himself.

The emotionally immature are incapable of this act of equation. They consider themselves superior, and to confirm to themselves this opinion they must display their superiority. Among the unconscious ways in which they do this are tactlessness and rudeness. By treating the other person as an inferior, they are able to conceal to themselves their own inferiority, inadequacy, and insecurity. They make themselves feel more important. In their own immaturity it is thus imperative to their egos that they treat others as inferiors.

It takes no personal development nor stature to be tactless or inconsiderate. Such behavior is nothing more than immaturity seeking expression. It is an unconscious effort to conceal or "cover-up" our sense of inferiority and of inadequacy. At its worse, perhaps, it is an expression of our failure to accept the dignity of the human personality, or of our unwillingness because of self-conceit to equate others with ourselves.

The mature person, on the other hand, lives on the level of human equation. He need not belittle someone in order to make himself an equal. He has the sense of adequacy within himself. He needs no false props to bolster his sense of importance. He has no need for wealth, social standing, position, or authority to give him stature, nor does he need to use these to show his superiority. Since he has reverence for his own inherent dignity he need not be irreverent of the dignity of others, nor tactless and rude in violating it.

It takes a man to be tactful and considerate as a way of life in dealing with his fellow men. It is not boys' play, nor is it for those laden with inferiority or hostility complexes. It is for the mature man, who is confident and secure in himself, who fully recognizes and accepts the innate dignity of all men, and who finds it inherently satisfying to relate himself helpfully and pleasingly to his fellow human beings.

THE SHAPING OF OUR DESTINY

Every man is responsible for his own destiny. The responsibility is his job, and the sooner he learns this fact, the sooner he will start thinking and acting like a self-reliant human being.

An individual must accept the fact that it is up to him to control and shape the forces that make his life. No one outside of himself has the obligation to shape these for him. It is he, himself, who is at the helm, and if he does not reach his desired destination, it is largely because he did not take full command.

If he does not assume full responsibility the world will shape his destiny for him, not according to his needs, potentialities, and ideals, but according to its own whims. It has a way of letting those flounder about aimlessly who wait for other men or for forces outside of themselves to mark the course of their lives for them.

He who, on the other hand, takes full control, finds both the inanimate world and the race of men willing and ready to cooperate with him, or at least to yield the way to him. It is he, however, who must set the goals, make the decisions, and do the things required. The world does not yield the right of way to substitute performers.

Unfortunately, however, we seem to be drifting rapidly into a philosophy of letting substitutes take charge. Too many of us rely on others to do our thinking and acting for us. Far too many of us do little more than float with the stream, relying on others to clear the path of whatever flotsam and jetsam are obstructing our passage or threatening to wreck our craft. Few of us groove channels for ourselves, and fewer still dare pilot our own way through them.

Somehow or other we are losing sight of the fact that our destinies are individual things, and that it is up to us personally to take charge and shape them according to our capacities, needs, and ideals. They cannot be handed over to an assembly line and come out tailor-made to fit us. They must be designed and hammered out by each one of us individually.

Each one of us is born to shape a destiny for himself. To allow forces outside of ourselves to shape them for us is to surrender our birthright as individual human personalities.

". . . BY THE SWEAT OF YOUR BROW"

The earth gives its fruits only to those who labor for them.

Its soil, and its waters, and its skies are rich in their abundance with the things that man needs and desires. But man must pay the price in effort to obtain them.

If he wishes the soil of the earth to yield potatoes, he must prepare it, plant potatoes, cultivate, and harvest them.

If he desires the gold, and silver, and copper, and ore hidden in its rocky interior, he must dig for them.

If he wants the fish from the seas, the grapes from the vineyards, the fruits from the orchards, the honey from the beehives—if he wishes these for the needs and comforts of himself and his loved ones, he must pay in terms of labor.

"To earn your bread by the sweat of your brow" is not a myth. It is a cold, hard reality. It applies to all. Whether we choose to be in the home, office, factory, or field—whether we cook meals, keep books, make automobiles, or sell insurance, the common denominator for success is work.

Without it man loses his vision, his confidence, and his enthusiasm. His life becomes largely meaningless.

On the other hand, there is no other preventative or cure so effective for boredom and fatigue, or for many of our mental and emotional ills, as an honest day's work every working day of the year.

There is no limit to the rich things that we may have—material, mental, spiritual—if we work hard enough to obtain them.

Know what you want! Work for it—and the earth will yield its treasures to you!

One of the fallacies common in the thinking of man is that his failure to succeed or to obtain happiness is the result of the circumstances in which his life is cast.

We do not like to think of failure as being a result of our own weaknesses, faults, or inadequacies. It hurts our pride to admit, even to ourselves, that it is not life, or fate, or to a large extent any of the forces outside of us, but rather our own short comings that defeat us.

It is true that man may be handicapped by hereditary or environmental factors over the making of which he had no control. A family background of poverty, lack of education, absence of social standing, or prevalency of low ideals and moral standards places obstacles in the course of development that are difficult to overcome. So, too, is it hard to rise above such personal impediments as sickness, poor training and education, lack of opportunities, and insufficient money. Financial and social occurrences such as depressions and wars also seriously hinder him.

But the significant thing is that many men overcome these obstructions, and rise to a glorious success and happiness. And it is only reasonable to assume if some men can do this, that it must be within the power of the human being as such to shape the vicissitudes of his life to his own ends, and to rise to victory through his difficulties, or in spite of them.

Students have long realized that it is not circumstances or obstacles that defeat man, but that it is rather how he ap proaches them and reacts to them. If he faces them with an attitude of defeatism, and permits them to control him, his failure is inevitable. If, on the other hand, he meets them with courage and fortitude, and with the determination to conquer them and to rise above them, he may be confident of success.

In the eternal plan he is intended to be the master of his life. But he must gain mastery through his will to control the circumstances which surround him, regardless of how adverse they may be. Defeat or failure is what happens if he allows these conditions or vicissitudes to master him.

No, it is not our fathers, or grandfathers, or great-great grandfathers and mothers, and their weaknesses and sins that defeat us. It is not the stars, or fate, or the Creator who decrees our success or failure. It is not our background, or our poverty, or our lack of opportunity. It is we who do it ourselves.

If we succeed it is because we have developed the strength to control our lives and the circumstances in which they are cast. If we fail, "The fault, dear Brutus, is not in our stars, But in ourselves, that we are underlings."

THE GRAIN OF MUSTARD SEED

It is the grain of mustard seed that is the open sesame that unlocks our powers and sets them free to shape our dreams into concrete realities.

It is this grain of belief in ourselves that is the magic wand that turns the weak into the strong, the listless into the energetic, and the dabbler into the producer. It is a mighty force that overcomes weaknesses, goes through obstacles, and knows no frustrations.

Since few of us have the time or opportunity to study the intricacies of this mighty force, it is fortunately not necessary that we do so in order to make it work effectively for us in the shaping of our lives. To make use of it fully, however, we must believe that faith in ourselves is a power that works miracles, and secondly we must put this faith to work in our daily lives by forming the habit of belief in ourselves.

That faith works is an inescapable fact. Too much evidence has accumulated in the verification of this fact to leave room for doubt. Not only have the great teachers and wise men consistently taught it and confirmed it by their deeds, but the experiences of the human race at large have also given empirical proof of it. When we are in doubt of its efficacy we need but remind ourselves of the simple, direct, unequivocal faith that was in the hearts of those who reached out into the unknown to do the impossible miracles known to man as happenings above and beyond the natural order of life and of the working of the universe. Instances of these are the miracles recorded in the New Testament.

In order to form the habit of believing in ourselves which is the second step in using the power of faith, the essential matter is that we act as if we did believe in ourselves. The outward act performed continuously and often enough will eventually result in a deep inner belief in ourselves.

To act with belief we must cut doubt and misgivings out of our minds. We must begin every intended achievement with the acceptance of the fact that it will be accomplished. To make faith work we must not give mental recognition to the possibility of defeat or frustration. Concepts of doubt and faith are incongruous. If doubt is present, there cannot be faith.

Let us proceed blindly in faith, if we must, but let there be no uncertainty in our thoughts as to our ability to accomplish successfully what we set out to do or as to the outcome of our strivings. Nor let there be any uncertainty in our minds regarding the untapped powers lying within us ready to be used if the need arises.

Faith works! And he who acts as if he believed in himself, keeping his mind free of doubt and misgivings, will work miracles as surely as night follows day. The grain of mustard seed is one of the most powerful forces on earth—ours to use for a better life.

If we wish to make ourselves more successful, we must begin the process of growth and development from the point at which we are at the present moment.

To grow means to evolve into something bigger and better. It means to further our development through a re-organization or extension of our activities. It means that we do the things that will make us stronger and more effective, and that will propel us to the goal we wish to accomplish.

All change or growth, however, must begin from the basis of our present strengths and weaknesses. A very common deterrent to growth or success is that we set for ourselves a goal, and then unfortunately act as if we had already reached it. We act as if what we would like to be or do had already become an accomplished fact. We act very much like the adolescent boy who transfers to himself the maturity of his father, but who has not yet had the benefit of the years of experience, and growth, and seasoning that makes for maturity.

Many of us have a tendency to do this in our jobs. In place of beginning wherever we are, and with what we have, and then slowly and painfully developing into what we would like to be, we let our minds trick us. Somehow or other we let our minds identify us with the finished goal, and cause us to act as if we had already reached it.

The result is that we remain mediocre or fail. Since in our thinking we have already identified ourselves with success, we make no progress, simply because we neglect to do the things necessary to bring fulfillment. We do nothing to develop the basic skills, talents, and working habits that are necessary for growth.

It is obvious, for instance, that we cannot reach executive stature by thinking or pretending that we are already competent and successful executives. Nor can we become competent doctors, or lawyers, or businessmen, unless at sometime we start where we are as untrained and unskilled neophytes, and go through the slow and detailed process of development of ourselves into competency and excellency.

We cannot become skilled workers, good fathers and mothers, successful salesmen, competent executives, or for that matter successful business institutions, unless at some time we face ourselves and make an accountancy of our abilities and deficiencies. This is the first step. It is like the financial statement of a business, except that it is a statement of personal assets and liabilities. To improve or to succeed means to proceed on the basis of this statement, and not on the basis of what the statement would be if we were highly successful and accomplished. To act as if we had already gained competency and stature greater than our statement of assets and liabilities indicates, is a delusion that leads to certain failure.

Let us face ourselves. Let us make a true statement of our strengths and weaknesses as they are at the present moment. Then let us take the second step, and proceed from there to develop ourselves into the individuals or organizations that are the realizations of our visions. The time to act like successful men and institutions is when we have achieved success.

TODAY, NOT TOMORROW

Man acts as if he had unlimited time.

The real fact is that he has very little of it. Time is a gift that embraces an instant. There is no promise of its extension even for a moment.

The only time man actually has to make something of himself is right now.

If he wants to assure himself that his life will be what he wants it to be, he must make it so at this moment—not this afternoon or tomorrow or ten years from now.

For all practical purposes, however, it is sensible for man to envision his life in day-long units. Among other things, it makes a convenient division in which is contained the gamut of life's experiences.

Each morning is a beginning in which he can start anew regardless of how badly he may have failed on the preceding day. Each night, too, is a finale which ends his inefficiencies and blunders, and brings nearer the hope of another dawn and the chance to try again, wiser by the experiences of the previous day.

A period of one day, too, is short enough so he can, within its duration, adhere to any resolutions of greater effort or of self-discipline. There are few things so difficult that he cannot follow through with them for at least a one-day period.

It is to make the greatest use of today—each day—that is man's best possible assurance that he will make out of his life what he most wants it to be.

The stuff that his life is made up of is what he thinks, and says, and does right now—today. Of what good are his intentions and resolutions for tomorrow, if tomorrow does not come? Even if a hundred or a thousand tomorrows come, his intentions will have little bearing on them unless he has molded his life today according to their pattern. He is tomorrow what he ends up with today.

Whatever, then, man wishes with certainty to become or to accomplish, he must be or do today. If he wishes to live graciously, charitably, and justly, he must of necessity be gracious, and charitable, and just today in his every thought and action.

If he wishes to be successful in his trade or profession, he must today acquire the knowledge, develop the skill, and perform the activities that make his success. To escape from these by way of good intentions for tomorrow does not count. It is merely setting a pattern of escape for his future conduct. He does tomorrow what he has schooled himself to do today.

It is today that we must, as employers, respect the human dignity of those who are employed by us. It is today that we must be the good spouse, the companion of our children, the loyal and dependable worker, the aggressive salesman, the courteous and helpful businessman, the devoted church member, the considerate and sympathetic friend and fellow human being.

Tomorrow does not exist. It is only today that is a reality. If we are to dream of having success and happiness, we must do today that which makes such success and happiness.

FIRST, LET US LOOK WITHIN

We don't get along well with the other fellow?

In that case it is an excellent bet that we, too, are not getting along well with ourselves.

It is quite possible that we don't get along with him because we see our hostile selves in him. We transfer to him our own attitudes and feelings. We project to him our insecurities, inferiorities, and hostilities. As a result we act toward him in the light of ourselves, and we get back from him exactly what we have projected to him.

In our relationships with him we thus literally fight ourselves. We are, let us say, unfriendly within us so we see unfriendliness in him. We lack trustworthiness and as a result we cannot trust him. We feel insecure, so we see hostility in him and give fight to it. We are filled with envy and aggressiveness project them to him, and then contend against them in our relationships.

Unconscious though this projection is, it vitiates our relationships. Nor can they be bettered until we change ourselves— "the one in whose image we recast the other person."

We had better look to ourselves first, then, if our relationships are unsatisfactory It is not always the other person who is wrong. The fault may lie within ourselves.

This, of course, does not imply that all our poor human relationships are brought about by the fact that we are inwardly at odds with ourselves or with life. It is possible that the under lying cause may be that we have not acquired the external skills of communicating ourselves to others. Or it could be that the other person is at fault either in his projection of himself or in his lack of personality skills.

It does suggest, however, that our relationship could be unsocial and hostile because we are in conflict with the image of ourselves that we have projected to the other person. The remedy for such a condition is obvious. It is to clean house within ourselves, or perhaps, to renovate our inner selves. This requires the up-rooting of our destructive thoughts, feelings, and attitudes, and the replacing of them with those that make for security, confidence, self-reliance, self-worth, and inner peace.

The first step in the betterment of our human relationships seem obviously to look within ourselves. The malignancies which are the root of the conflict in our relationships with others could possibly be our own.

A MORE PLEASANT JOURNEY

Life is too short a journey not to make it as pleasant as possible.

Nothing will brighten it more than to travel in a manner that merits for us the affection and good will of our fellow travelers.

It is the good will given to us spontaneously from the hearts of others because of the way in which we relate ourselves to them that is the precious ingredient of a happy and deeply satisfying journey through life. It is the good will and the little demonstrations of affection genuinely given to us because we have contributed something of importance to the lives of others that is the spice that gives savor to the pleasures of the journey.

Such giving of good will to us is something, however, that is won by us. It is the natural result of a relationship between ourselves and our fellow men that adds something to their sense of importance, their security, their faith and courage, and to their sense of adequacy.

Strangely enough, it is through our simple everyday relationships that we make these contributions to others. It is by being friendly to them, not now and then, but all of the time so they can depend upon our friendliness. It is by smiling warmly whenever we meet them, thus reassuring them, or perhaps dispelling their loneliness, uncertainty, or insecurity.

It is by being helpful whenever a lift from us could make life easier or more pleasant for them. It is by going out of our way to aid them when trouble strikes or when problems become too burdensome. It is by giving them a verbal pat on the back when they are depressed, or a word of encouragement in periods of self-doubt or discouragement.

It is by confirming their feeling of being somebody in giving recognition to their interests, their opinions, their beliefs, their joys, and their problems. It is by helping them think more highly of themselves through complimenting them on the things in which they excel or on that which they have accomplished. It is by respecting the importance of their ego, and by being forever watchful in word and deed not to deflate or wound that ego.

We merit their spontaneous good will by being courteous; by bearing with them in their deficiencies; by understanding that all human beings have their ups and downs, and thus not taking offense when occasionally they are out of mood.

Generally expressed, we contribute to others in ways that merit this good will and affection when we relate ourselves to them in our daily lives in a manner that feeds their intangible needs and hungers. It is doing to them what in our hearts we would like to have them do to us.

Nothing adds more to the pleasantness of our journey than does the good will and affection that flows to us spontaneously from the hearts of others because we do or have done these things to them.

WE MAKE IT BE

The lilting melody of a song popular at the time of this writing is bringing pleasure to millions of people. This is as it should be. It is a pleasing tune.

In addition to this pleasure given by its melody, the nostalgic title and refrain of the song seem to bring consolation both to older people whose lives have not fruited as expected in their youthful dreams, and to the young who unconsciously perhaps are seeking in advance an excuse for the possible mediocrity or failure of their future.

Any mature person, however, will hope that the philosophy expressed in its lyric will not be accepted seriously by too many of our young men and women.

The title and refrain of the song, "Whatever will be, will be," is not the credo of the man bent on making a success of his life and of shaping it according to his own dreams and aspirations.

The philosophy of the individual with a dream and a purpose is that it is up to him to make his future. The refrain in the song of his life is "Whatever we make it be, will be."

No one who has had the benefit of years of experience with life will deny that there are things favorable and unfavorable over which we have no control that will to some extent determine our future. But even in these matters it is not so much what happens to an individual as it is the reaction of the individual person to these things that is the vital element in the making of his future.

In the main, however, what the future will be is what we shape it into being. In a very real sense it is the product of causality. It is the effect or end result of how we have planned, and worked, and learned; of how we have developed our personal growth; of how we have reacted to the misfortunes and setbacks of life; and of how we have accepted and made the best of the opportunities that have come our way.

The future is somewhat like the end of a ball game. How it turns out depends on how well the preceding nine innings were played. Few games are won as a matter of luck. Many of them are lost, however, because of the deficiencies in training, discipline, teamwork, and skill of the players.

So it is with the future. What it will be for anyone of us will rarely be the result of luck or fate. It will be the product of our own efforts and disciplines, and everyone of us can largely shape it to his own liking.

Many of us are not successful in this because we do not know what we wish our future to be. We have never definitely visualized it. How can we create something about which we have no mental image? Equally as many of us fail because we have not taken charge of our lives. In a sort of a vague way we expect it to evolve itself through forces beyond our control. Or we look to others to shape it for us.

When tomorrow, or next year, or our whole future as such does not turn out as we expect it to, we blame destiny—"What will be, will be." What might be more honest would be to turn the spotlight on ourselves to see what we have done, and have not done, to have made of our lives such a mediocre and unglorified creation.

MENTALLY BEDRIDDEN

It is because we are mentally bedridden that we live such commonplace lives.

Our powers and faculties to do and accomplish are bogged down in the sloughs of our minds.

We fear to release our minds to explore the possibilities of their own wings. We imprison our thoughts and feelings within the confines of our daily routines. We do not set them free to explore the unaccustomed or to venture into the unfamiliar and unknown. The substance of it is that many of us because of lethargy, or fear, or mere habit do not allow our minds to reach beyond the point of our noses.

The effect on the caliber of our lives by this mental stalemate is far-reaching and tragic. And in no other way does this stalemate affect us more than in the use of our powers and faculties to do, to accomplish, and to find happiness.

A man's deeds can go only as far as the reaches of his thoughts and feelings. Action is nothing more than the effort "to actualize," or the effort to give concrete embodiment to, our thoughts and feelings. Without the preliminary mental visualization there is no craftsmanship; there is nothing to which to give shape, or nothing to accomplish. The thought or feeling must precede the act of creation.

It is because we fail to set free our thoughts and feelings that we do not discover the powers within us to create and accomplish. We thus live and die with our potentialities undiscovered and wasted.

But man can unchain his thoughts and feelings, and set them free. In fact, he must do so to discover the powers for accomplishment that are within him. The caliber of our thoughts and feelings is merely a habit, mostly developed unconsciously. We think and feel as we do, small or big, negatively or positively, restrictively or expansively according to the die in which our minds were cast by the thoughts and feelings to which we were exposed in our past experiences.

Our way of thinking and feeling is, consequently, not a measure of our minds. It is merely our minds operating in the set of a limited pattern designed by habit. The habit, on the other hand, is largely the result of that to which our environment has accustomed us. Its formation reaches back as far as to infancy and childhood, and to the mental patterns of our parents, teachers, and other associates. What it is at any given time is the product of all of our associations and experiences throughout the years.

To get a measure of our minds we must go beyond the acquired pattern. We must dare to do some thinking and feeling beyond our habitual way. We must break the shackles of habit and set our minds free. It is only then that we can find the creative potential of our minds, and can make use of the powers and faculties to do and accomplish that lie dormant within us.

To be mentally bedridden is, indeed, never to discover or to make use of our powers to arise to our full potential.

TENDING TO THE BUSINESS AT HAND

To keep his life reasonably ordered and satisfying each of us has need for all the time, energy, and wisdom available to him.

Living one's personal life is a full-time job. To do it satisfactorily has been the chief problem of individual man from the beginning of time. It has always been his most perplexing and evasive task.

One of the things man has learned in the struggle for an effective personal life is that it leaves no time nor energy to be critical of the ways in which other men try to fulfill their lives.

Unfortunately there are always a few of us who think that our way of living is superior to that of others. As a result we have the inclination to be critical of any way that is different from ours. We develop the tendency to advise others according to our thinking, and to foist our way upon them as superior and infallible.

The fallacy of thus remaking the lives of others according to our standards is two-fold. First, it implies the assumption that we have found the one correct way to the proper conduct of life. This is an assumption that the greatest of the philosophers and wise men of the ages have not dared to make. Its arrogance is phenomenal.

The other fallacy is that it assumes that all men are alike, and that what is satisfying and fulfilling for one is also so for the other person. It overlooks the fact that every human being is a separate and unique entity, and that as such his needs, tastes, beliefs, and values are different from those of any other person.

The simple fact is that there is no standard satisfaction for human strivings and yearnings. What is satisfying to one individual is not necessarily so for the other. That which feeds the needs of one may leave another famished.

Since the hungers and needs among individuals are as variegated as the shells on the beach, each person must himself find the way of life most satisfying to him. But the fact that he has found a way does not mean that it is also a satisfying way to other persons. Nor does it mean that it is the one correct way. There are literally as many correct ways as there are human beings, each according to his own nature and his own needs. The only common denominator of them is that they must operate within the moral framework of the universe.

Since we cannot put ourselves in the shoes of another, we should not be critical of his way of life. Nor will we have the time and energy to be so if we are tending fully to the business at hand, which is the shaping of our own life into a satisfying and fulfilling one. This in itself is a full-time job.

THE LIGHT OF OUR SHADOW

Probably not one of us will in our lifetime accomplish something so spectacular that it will vitally change the mode of living of mankind.

We will not make a great discovery, invent an ingenious machine, compound a Salk formula, write an immortal book, or lead a nation to peace and prosperity.

All of us, however, have it in our power to do that which is of even greater importance than the spectacular. We can make our daily lives a blessing to our fellow men. We can so live, paraphrasing the words of the poet Gibran, "that our shadow will be a light upon the faces of our fellow human beings" whenever and wherever we come in contact with them. We can by being lovingly creative in our relationships raise the tone or quality of the lives of all with whom we have even a moment of association.

We are creative when we bring into existence anything that has not been present before, either by influencing or modifying that which already exists, or by starting anew from the foundation.

To paint a beautiful picture is to create, but it is no more so than to cause a smile to come to a child's lips, to change an attitude, to impart an ideal, to change the quality of the day for someone through a pleasant greeting, to bring a spark of courage to a heart belabored with despair or defeat, or to bring about a moment of happiness.

But to have these masterpieces of our daily creativeness

cast the full splendor of light on our fellow men, and on our own hearts, we must do them lovingly.

To do them lovingly means to do them for their own sake— without seeking or expecting anything in return for ourselves. We do them simply because they add something, be it ever so small or large, of good, beauty, or well-being to the life of someone else.

Loving-creativeness is a way of life in which forgetting about ourselves, we do the little human things that for a moment brighten the way for the individual at hand, and make his journey a more fulfilling and satisfying one.

It is no more than the giving of a little bit of ourselves in being pleasant, kindly, and thoughtful in our daily relationships, without regard to whom they are, rich man or pauper, saint or sinner, child or adult, boss or custodian. It costs us nothing. It requires little effort. But as a way of life it makes our presence on earth a blessing to our fellow men, and a rich meaningful adventure to ourselves.

No, few of us will accomplish spectacular things. All of us, however, can spectacularly affect the quality of the lives of other human beings by relating ourselves to them in a lovingly creative way. All of us can if we wish through our simple daily relationships live so that "our shadow will be a light upon the lives" of our fellow sojourners.

PERHAPS, A LITTLE LOUSE

If we could see ourselves objectively we might be more than a little surprised at how different we are from the self-conceived image we have of ourselves.

Some of us conceivably could have a pleasant surprise in store for us. We do not all have a picture of ourselves that is in line with our real worth. Some few of us think less of ourselves than we should. As a rule, however, most of us would be unpleasantly shocked in seeing how different we are in some less flattering ways from our self-conceived image.

It is only natural that we see ourselves subjectively. Every individual looks not only at himself but also at all other aspects of life from his particular point of view. It is for him the only possible point of observation. When, however, we thus view ourselves nature makes use of some subtle trickery. As a result we do not see ourselves as we actually are, but rather as we look perched high on a pedestal of our own making. Perhaps nature thus designs to protect our egos. The result too frequently, however, is that we look much better to ourselves than we do to the objective observer who sees us from a level point of view.

We could to some extent correct the distortion of our picture of ourselves by making allowance for our unavoidable human tendency of elevating ourselves. Better still, however, would be to discard from our minds the preconceived notion of personal perfection. Such perfection is simply not consistent with human nature, and to think that we are perfectly whole and sound borders on nothing less than arrogance.

All of us have our weaknesses and faults. They are not necessarily serious ones, but they are defections, and any defection interferes to some extent in the successful unfoldment of our lives. Among other things, is the fact that it in some way, perhaps only in a minor manner, throws out of harmony our relations with our fellow men.

The defection could be some casual matter as a carelessness in personal appearance; or it could be a more serious unfavorable personality trait such as inconsiderateness or tactlessness. Again it could be an emotional immaturity as the inability to face reality; or it could be a serious moral deficiency such as an absence of a sense of justice. Whatever it is, it is important that we realize that it could be a part of our own personal makeup unnoticed when we look at ourselves subjectively, but prominent to the eyes of those who see us objectively.

Some of us probably would make decided changes in ourselves if we could see ourselves as others see us. All of us, perhaps, would strut a little less, and be more inclined to walk with greater humility among our fellow men.

The great Scottish poet Robert Burns expressed it immortally in "To a Louse." During a church service the poet sat behind an elegantly dressed and highly refined lady, evidently conscious of her own superiority. From the poet's vantage point of observation, however, his attention was distracted from the elegance before him to a little louse crawling on the lady's bonnet. He exclaimed:

> O wad some Pow'r the giftie gie us
> To see oursels as others see us!
> It wad frae mony a blunder free us,
>   And foolish notion:
> What airs in dress an' gait wad lea'e us,
>   And e'en devotion!

No doubt the best of us have at least one little louse meandering about on our highly rated selves.

47

THE NEED TO BE OURSELVES

One of the most tragic mistakes man makes is to strive to be what some other person is.

To emulate another man's virtues is wisdom. To try to fit ourselves into his shoes, however, is folly.

No two human beings are exactly alike, and no wishing or effort can make them alike. They are individual persons, each of a separate die, and each of a specific role to play in the unfoldment of creation. Their physical inheritances are different; their aptitudes and capacities are singular and distinctive; their emotional reactions vary, if not in kind, at least in degree.

As futile as it is to try to be that which by nature we are not designed to be, so it is, on the other hand, the way to personal growth and realization to strive to be one's self. The salvation of man lies in the effort he makes to reach his own potential best in the die in which nature has formed him.

The capacities, skills, and specific accomplishments of others do not concern him as avenues or goals for the unfoldment of himself. Self-unfoldment must always be in line with his own capacities and other individual potentialities.

Not all men, for instance, can become outstanding businessmen, nor can such businessmen by virtue of the particular capacity that made them successful in business become as much as mediocre philosophers. To become a skilled accountant, physician, scientist, mechanic, or social service worker requires the corresponding talent. This talent is inborn. It cannot be acquired through willing or through effort.

One reason we wish so often to become some other person is that we see him only from the viewpoint of accomplishment in his vocational specialty. We do not see him totally. The result is that in place of striving to be ourselves in the particular area that makes us distinctive and outstanding, we waste our energies and powers in trying to become what we were not designed to be.

Not as categorically, but nevertheless in a large measure the same is true of likes, tastes, and sense of values. These, too, cannot be exactly like those of another person, nor would we want them to be. Each individual has his own, finely wrought by the myriad of experiences that have made him what he personally is. As long as these are not socially harmful the individual should lay claim to them as expressions of himself. He need not apologize for them nor be envious of those of others. Who is so qualified as to be the arbiter of human tastes and values? Who but the individual can decide for himself which is of the higher order of things—pig hocks or lamb shanks?

To be one's potential best self: — that is the sensible goal of individual striving. And, it is a workable one if man does his utmost in the particular circumstances and environment of his life. On the other hand, to try to be someone else is both an unattainable end and a denial of one's stature and dignity as an individual entity with a particular creative purpose.

PAY FOR IT—TAKE IT

God's world is a bountiful world—rich beyond measure.

It is, too, our world, freely given to us as the setting in which to evolve our lives according to our desire. Its abundance, far beyond our needs and wants, is ours for the taking, provided only that we pay the small price asked, according to known terms and in the proper coin.

The terms for helping ourselves to this abundance are simple, but iron clad. There are no exceptions. They are simply that we pay in advance. Would we have success, honor, or riches? Would we be needed among men and respected by them? Would we have contentment, wisdom, and peace of heart? "Pay for it, and take it," said the great American Ralph Waldo Emerson.

But pay for it we must, and in advance. There is no advance return on contemplated future performances. There is no taking on the basis of good intentions. It is only the coins we have placed in the till that count, but there is no limit to the number we deposit nor to their value. We pay according to our desires, and take to our heart's content.

And what are the proper coins that are accepted for barter? They are simply ways of life, and among the most important of them are sincerity of purpose; honesty of effort; the desire to be useful; devotion to duty; just and compassionate relationship with our fellow men; faith in ourselves and in God. These are the coins to be placed in the till as prepayment. Each of them is of great value on its own; but priceless when smelted together with the others into one coin: an amalgamation that becomes the way of our daily life.

Many of us fail because we want to get the blessings of life on our terms and in our coin. We want them on the basis of what we think we must do to obtain them. We try to get them our way, and at exorbitant prices. Too frequently we go on the assumption that we must slave for them, fight for them, cringe in suppliance for them. Too frequently our belief seems to be that we can get them only in the face of overwhelming odds against us; that life is unwilling, moody, niggardly.

If our experience with life has been that it is miserly and unyielding, it is perhaps that we have sought to deal with it the hard way—our way in place of its way. We have substituted our opinion of how to reap from it an abundant harvest for the universal law by which it undeviatingly operates.

Many of us expect the windows of heaven to open without effort on our part. Equally as many, if not more, expect to pry open these munificent windows through tireless effort alone. But neither method is according to the law as experienced by those who have had the gifts of heaven showered upon them.

Effort is an inherent part of the law, but it is not the whole law. Effort must be sustained effort. It must be directed toward a useful purpose. It must be for the accomplishment of a service for mankind. It must be in harmony with the rights and well-being of fellow human beings. And it must be deeply rooted in faith in our ability to do, and faith in God's desire for man to make his life a rich and satisfying one.

If we would share to our heart's content in the abundance of life, the secret of doing so is a simple one. We pay the price, and then help ourselves. It is ours to take. But pay in advance we must, and in stipulated coin of the universal realm.

51

THE WALLS WE BUILD AROUND US

To reach beyond ourselves is a principle of life that is among the most critical in consequences of those experienced by the human race.

Upon whether we follow it as individual persons depends whether our lives will be rich or barren. And upon how many of us follow it depends the future of the human race. A race of individuals solely self-centered could not long survive.

The great human tragedy is that so many of us cheat ourselves out of the full possible richness of our lives simply because we will not learn the importance of reaching out beyond ourselves. In place of it we do that which on the surface looks like the more natural thing. We build walls around ourselves, and live and strive directly in terms of the needs and desires of that which is within our own enclosure and pertains to us. We concern ourselves little or none with the needs of the men and women who lie outside of our walls.

Unconsciously we human beings are forever building walls of this kind, little or big, around ourselves and ours. We build fences marking off our personal domains from those of humanity at large. We make islands of self-interest out of what is ours, and lose concern for the other human islands that surround us, except perhaps when we find use of them for our own aggrandizement.

We do this in spite of the fact that historical experience has shown that no man can live fully and richly with an enclosure about him and his. Man obviously cannot do this for the reason that he is not created an isolated being who can find full satisfaction in self-directed activity. He is an integral part of the larger body of mankind. Because of his nature as a human being he cannot compartmentalize that which is of concern to him and his, and ignore the strivings, the needs, the sufferings, the dreams, and the aspirations of his fellows. At least he cannot do so if he wishes to have more than an abortive life and a sickly, twisted emotional and spiritual self.

To live fully and richly it is, of course, not required of man that he deny himself the satisfaction of his own needs. Neither is it necessary that he curtail his personal advancement. But it is required that he does not stop at that point. He must reach beyond himself and his needs. His life belongs not solely to himself and to those he has walled in with him. It belongs to all men and for its fulfillment it depends on all men. If he would play the part of a man and develop into fulness his potentially rich life, he must tear down the artificial walls he has erected and must enlarge the area of his concern to others as well as himself.

To fence himself off with walls from the parent body of humanity is to sever the artery of vital supply between himself and the source of his richest nourishment. Any kind of wall he erects between himself and his fellow men constricts the artery of supply ever so little or so much. It shuts off the flow of that by which he grows into the fruition of his richest and fullest self.

To live fully and completely as men and women we must tear down the walls that separate us from full participation in the lives of our fellow men.

JUST BEING NICE TO PEOPLE

Time and time again in business and in personal life we see the rewards that come from just being nice to people.

Most of us are so hurried by the details of the day's work that we don't think of taking the little time needed to be thoughtful and considerate of others. We are so preoccupied by the mechanics of the job that we fail to be tactful, and gracious, and helpful.

Yet it is these acts of being nice that cause people to feel kindly and to show favor to us. It is the moments we take to be friendly, to be a little extra helpful, or to say a word of praise, or of sympathy, or of encouragement, that frequently make for us the best friends and supporters.

It can quite possibly be that these little moments and acts are the deciding factor in getting for us some extra consideration that will close a sale in our favor, or win a promotion for us. But what is most important is that they are the ones that will earn for us the devotion and good will of others.

And it is this very thing—the good will and devotion of others—that all of us need more than anything else if we wish to be successful either as individuals or as a business organization. We cannot operate alone; we must accomplish through others, and we are dependent on their feelings towards us.

As individuals we can never function entirely by ourselves. All our acts are in relationship to some other person or persons, and their outcome is determined in some measure, large or small, by that person's willingness or unwillingness to have us succeed in those actions. We have others working for us, or against us, and it is up to us to determine which way it will be.

As business organizations, too, we have the same situation, except that the relationships are multiplied. We have more people to deal with, more people whose loyalty and good will we must win to our side, if we wish to succeed.

But in both instances, we know that the most effective way of winning people to wish good for us, and to act for our good, is to be nice to them. It is to be nice not just to the few whom we approve or favor, but to all with whom we have association of any kind.

To be friendly, tactful, helpful, and gracious to all with whom we come in contact, that is the trick. To take a moment to be nice to people wherever we meet them; to give them a little extra measure of thoughtfulness, and consideration, and appreciation—it is this that returns good will and devotion to us in overflowing measure.

THE PATHETIC FALLACY

It is still a too common opinion among us that good human relations is synonymous with weakness and sentimentality in dealing with our fellow men. We think of it as characteristic of the dreamer and idealist, but unsuited for the man of action, the doer of deeds.

To get people to do our bidding, the thinking is that we must act with authority and finality. The persuader we must hold before them is the specter of fear. They do as we bid, or face the consquences of our displeasure. Essentially, the method believed in is one of force—the force of our greater importance and the power to make it felt.

What a pathetic fallacy such thinking is! What a manifestation it is of our immaturity and lack of experience! What a sad expression it is of our lack of understanding of human nature!

No one will question that in certain circumstances men can be forced through fear to do our bidding. But to believe that they can be motivated more strongly by it, than by creating in them through our good human relationships the desire to cooperate fully with us, borders on childish thinking.

Men who do things because of fear are slaves. They work and act as slaves. They do what they have to do to save themselves from the lash, and no more. They are driven, not motivated.

We drive animals, perhaps; but we motivate men by persuasion. Man is not a brute creature. He acts not merely to get food and drink, and to avoid pain. Man is of a different ilk.

He has internal hungers and needs as well. It is to find satisfactions for these that is the mainspring to action for him.

To feed these hungers is to persuade man into his highest activity and into his fullest cooperation with our aims. But it is not by force that we persuade. It is not by parading our importance. It is not by impressing him with our authority. It is not by commanding him.

We persuade man rather by relating ourselves to him in a manner that recognizes his importance, that adds to his security, that shows respect for his individuality, that gives identity to him as a person. We persuade him when we help him through our relationships to realize himself as a person and to grow more fully within the limits of his capacity.

There is nothing theoretical, soft, or sentimental about such a relationship. It is strictly a matter of understanding the nature of a human personality, and of having the maturity to be able to act accordingly.

Nor is it the easy, softer course of action. It takes little self-knowledge to know how much more difficult it is, for instance, to give recognition than to grasp it for ourselves; to help the other person to feel important than to parade our own importance; to let others do things their way than do them our way; to be understanding than to be intolerant.

It is much more the test of a man to be friendly, kindly, considerate, and courteous than it is to throw around among people the weight of his superior self.

THE PRICELESS FIFTY-ONE HOURS

It is the element of time out of which the stuff of life is made.

Everything that we do should be considered in terms of time. It is the limited and irreplaceable ingredient of life. Each one of us has a specific amount measured out to us, and as it ticks away moment by moment the remaining amount left becomes less and less. We have only so much of it, and what has been spent cannot be recovered or replaced.

If we have wasted money, we can earn more to take its place. If we have used or lost material possessions, we can replace them. But time is different. It cannot be created, nor is there a reservoir from which we can draw more of it. It does not exist in the past nor in the future. It is only now.

But the human being goes through life wasting it as if there were no end to the supply. Since it is not something tangible that he can take in his hands and feel it or see it, it is immaterial to him. He does not think of it as something that is concrete and substantial. Yet it is the only thing that is essentially vital to him.

Strange to say, many of us do not try to schedule or control it except in a general way in relation to our working day. We think of the day in terms of the eight hours we spend on the job. When we speak of having a hard day tomorrow, we think of an eight-hour period in terms of a full day. We do not seem to be conscious of the fact that a day is a twenty-four-hour period and not an eight-hour one.

What happens to the other sixteen hours? We must sleep, of course. If we are growing children, or adults with special needs, we require eight hours or more. Many of us, however, waste the precious substance of time in excessive sleep because we are bored with life. We have no interests to keep us awake.

Eating, dressing, and transportation, too, take their required toll of time. But if we were to allow the generous amount of three hours for these, plus eight hours for sleep, we still would have for our exclusive personal use five hours a day, plus an additional eight hours each for Saturday and Sunday, a total of fifty-one hours a week. This is eleven hours more than we have in an average work week.

We believe it would be safe to say that much of this we consume by just sitting and thinking about something to do with these hours. Others are wasted by waiting for the time to come to go to work, to eat, or to go to bed. They become wasted hours, because they are not planned ones. We do not look upon them as part of our day.

Yet it is in these hours that we must do the real carving out of our lives. They are the hours that are particularly our own to satisfy our needs for love, self-improvement, culture, play, worship, and service. They are the decisive hours because it is in these that we must create our own personal lives into the particular pattern to which we individually aspire.

LET'S COUNT OUR BLESSINGS

Many of us have developed the habit of looking at the adverse side of life, and to lay undue stress on those exceptional incidents that cause us inconvenience, discomfort, or unhappiness.

We permit these distressing conditions or circumstances to color our entire outlook, and to cause us to judge life in terms of the isolated, unfavorable things, rather than of the more usual and favorable ones. The cost of this to us in the loss of personal happiness, enthusiasm, and contentment is probably beyond measure. It brings about an attitude of futility, and a feeling of depression and helplessness that often makes life a burden, rather than a challenge and a joy.

It must be admitted that life has its problems and difficulties, and that it can at times be very ruthless. But these distresses and problems are exceptions, for their number is insignificant when compared with the blessings that are a part of the warp and woof of each day.

But to recognize and appreciate these blessings we must develop an "awareness" of them. We must develop the habit of seeing that which is the norm, rather than that which is the exception. We must learn to respond to the flowers in our garden, rather than to concentrate on the few weeds we do not like.

Fortunately, there is a very simple way in which we can develop this "awareness," and thereby raise the caliber of our life to one of confidence, joyousness, and challenge.

It is the simple practice of counting our blessings as opposed to our tribulations or afflictions. Let us list them on a sheet of paper divided into two columns; one for the afflictions, and the other for the blessings that are ours. It is amazing how few are the afflictions or negative factors that one can list. On the other hand, it is even more astonishing how many are the blessings, any one of which would make life worth-while.

Let's count our blessings, or at least a few of the hundreds of things that life benignly gives us, often without effort on our part—things that mean so much to us that they are priceless.

Here are a few of the blessings that are common to most of us: The woman who is our mate; our children, and all the happy memories they have given us; our job, our home, the good health of our family; our food, clothing, educational opportunities, recreational facilities, our freedom of religion, the nearness of our temples of worship; our unlimited opportunities for success and advancement, our democratic way of life and form of government; all the good friends we have; the song of the meadowlark; the beauty of this November day; the illimitable sky at night; our comforts and conveniences; the excellent available medical care; and so on, and on, and on. There is hardly a limit to them.

So let's count our blessings—put them down on paper—and we will probably find a new kind of life, one full of confidence, and faith, and enthusiasm, and promise.

THE IRREDUCIBLE MINIMUM

Many, many centuries ago in the early dawn of civilization there was formulated for mankind a code of living.

It was made up of certain principles that, based upon man's created nature, were to serve him as an irreducible minimum of conduct—if he wished to live well and happily.

These principles were not arbitrary dictates devised by some tyrannical power. They were rather an expression to man by his Creator saying in so many words: "I created you according to a certain design to live happily and effectively. I guarantee that you will accomplish this if you live according to the nature of this being that I have created. Here are the few simple things that you must and must not do. Follow these, and you will realize yourself. Live according to them, and your life will be well. Ignore them—or any one of them—and you will, by going contrary to your own nature, invite disaster."

This code of living is the Moral Law. Often it is referred to as The Decalogue, or the Ten Commandments. Simply stated, it tells us that we must not hurt our fellow man needlessly—that we must treat him as we would like him to treat us. And that is all.

We cannot, for instance, take undue advantage of him; we cannot deceive him or misguide him; we cannot deprive him of what is rightfully his; we cannot infringe on his rights and privileges; we cannot violate his dignity as an individual.

The Moral Code is an emphasis on the fundamental necessity of integrity in any successful way of living. We must live in a specified moral framework. The fundamental and all-important issue in each life is that of integrity. He whose thoughts and actions are outside of the periphery of this Code cannot hope for fulfillment of himself. This has been confirmed and verified by the historical records of man, and thus for thousands of years both individuals and nations have borne out in their lives the wisdom of abiding by the principles of integrity.

And on the positive side of the minimum we must actually help man to confirm himself in his rights.

That's it, simple but effective. It is the law of one's own being. Follow it, and it means fulfillment; disregard it, and it means disaster. It is the irreducible minimum.

ACCEPTING OR REJECTING WISDOM

It is an historical experience that mankind has always been slow and seemingly reluctant to make application of the great teachings of its wise men.

This is so, perhaps, because of man's tendency to look upon as theoretical anything he cannot see, or touch, or in any way physically apprehend. Or again it may be so because of his proclivity to look upon guidance and direction as applicable to the other person but not to himself. He may unconsciously have formed the conceit that he is perfection and is already an exemplification of that which is taught. Thus, in his mind, these teachings apply only to the other person who unfortunately, in his opinion, has not matured as he has.

Whatever the reason may be, we frequently make no effort actually to apply to our lives that which has been proved to be of great value to us, and in many instances could make the difference between happiness and unhappiness, between fulfillment and nonfulfillment.

An instance at point are the thoughts and emotions that we permit ourselves to entertain. From times back almost as far as recorded history goes, wise men and great teachers have told us that we cannot think and feel negatively and destructively, and yet live healthy, happy, and fulfilled lives. They have taught us that such thoughts and emotions not only destroy our relationships with others, but that they also incapacitate us who harbor them. Medical science of today has added its warnings against the bad effects of such thoughts and emotions on our physical well-being. It has told us with surprising exactness what glandular and other changes these bring about, and what the consequent ill effects are on our physical system.

In spite of all this, we continue to fear, to envy, to resent, to doubt, and to hate. We allow others to annoy us. We are fearful of life. We doubt the ultimate goodness of things. We hate those who slight us, and envy and resent those who seemingly do better than we are doing. We keep ourselves in a constant emotional turmoil because we do not like this or that, or because an associate acts immaturely, or differs from us in his beliefs and points of view, or because we are suspicious of the intentions of others. We are perpetually, it seems, under the tension of some conflict, or obstacle, or frustration.

The way out of it, the great teachers have told us, is a change of attitude simply through substitution. It is to replace these thoughts and emotions with those of courage, faith, serenity, kindliness, and tolerance. The human being, they tell us, cannot dwell on two thoughts or feelings at the same time. Thus the choice of which one he allows himself to entertain is his. The negative and destructive kind of thought and emotion will eventually make of him and his life a dwarfed and sickly thing. The other will bring health, success, and happiness.

Again it is a matter of accepting or rejecting for practical use that which the wise men have taught us for centuries.

TAKING LIFE TOO SERIOUSLY

Most of us could do a much better job of living effectively if we did not take life quite so seriously.

Life, of course, is a serious business. It imposes many responsibilities on us. It presents many problems. Every turn of the way has its trials, obstacles, and difficulties. There are, however, sensible limits to how far we must look upon these as important, and to what extent we must accept them as personal obligations.

There is no doubt, for instance, that accepting too seriously the things that are inevitable needlessly drains away from us much of the energy that could be used to make the best of what is within our control. All of us would be better off if we discarded the notion that we run the whole show of our lives. The fact is that we do not. There are forces beyond ourselves that play important parts in that show. To accept personal responsibility for the operations of these forces, or to be rebellious to their effect on our lives, is to take life too seriously. It is being foolhardy in our seriousness.

We also take life too seriously when we fail to distinguish between the things that are really important and those that are of little consequence. This applies both to our problems and difficulties, and to the things that we want for our well-being and happiness.

Most of our problems are not important ones. Many of them are of so little consequence in the totality of our lives that whether we find a solution for them or not is of little significance. By far the greatest number is nothing more than petty personal annoyances. To forget about them is frequently the best course of action.

So is it, too, with many of the things that we want or that we think we need for our well-being and happiness. Many of these are desirable, but their vital importance exists merely in our minds. Actually having them or not having them adds little to our life, nor detracts much from it. In our sense of values, to place these in the same category as we do the indispensable needs of life, such as health, means of a livelihood, companionship, love, honor, and peace of mind is to be facetiously too serious in our attitude toward life.

When we make the inevitable a matter of personal concern, or when we give the same weight to what is of little importance as we do to what is indispensable, we take life too seriously. In doing either, we foolishly waste energies that could be used to live more effectively.

THE BLACK SPOTS OR THE WHITE SURFACE?

It is said of a sales manager that during a particularly trying national economic period he called for a meeting of his salesmen from their far-flung territories.

In front of the assembly room he put a large white screen on which he placed a blot of black ink large enough to be plainly visible.

He asked his men to study the screen carefully and then tell him what they saw. One after another of them repeated that they saw a black spot. In spite of the manager's urging that they observe the screen more carefully, the men came up with the same answer: a black ink blot.

Finally, in desperation, the manager said: "All of you see the black blot on the surface, but does not one of you see the large white surface?"

So it is with many of us in our daily living. We are keenly sensitive to the black spots, but close our eyes to the predominately white surface.

Anyone who has passed beyond the fairyland of childhood knows that life has many black spots; that it has, in fact, a constant succession of them: disappointments, obstacles, and frustrations. They are part of its very fabric.

Too many of us, however, look upon life in terms of these spots. We are aware of them and nothing else. We concentrate on them to the extent that we lose sight of the predominate white surface.

Any realistic, even if cursory, examination of the happenings that make up our lives will show us, however, that this kind of perspective or outlook is plainly contrary to fact.

Life is predominately full of the things that favor us. It is abundantly rich in the good things it showers upon us. For every frustration or obstacle, it gives us a multiplicity of things that further our welfare and happiness. Life is meant to be the way of fulfillment for the human being. It is not designed to be an instrument for his destruction.

The trouble is with us and our outlook. It is not with life. We have permitted ourselves to be so blinded by the things that we do not like and by those that cause us annoyance that we become oblivious to the richness of the real warp and woof of life.

How often, for instance, do we think of the beauty of the earth in which we live or about the universe that surrounds us with all its forces and powers? Are these not a part of our lives? What about the food we eat? The clothes we wear? The homes that shelter us? The opportunity to work and make a living? Our wonderful bodies? Our health? The many courtesies and considerations, the understanding, and the sympathy that we receive from our acquaintances and associates?

What about our friendships and loves? Are these not much more vital and important than the obstacles and difficulties that beset our daily paths?

Perhaps a little less attention to the black spots, and a greater concentration on the big white surface, would make healthier and happier individuals out of most of us.

We live in an age of formulas, machine production, and speed. When we want something, someone among us finds a formula; another devises a machine according to the specifications of the formula; another pushes a button. And, then, lo and behold, like the jinni of the Arabian tales, what we want appears, be it a new kind of refrigerator for our kitchens or a rocket trip to the moon.

Unfortunately most of us have little or no part in creating the formulas, in inventing the machines, or in pushing the buttons that set them in motion. Creating and producing is done for us. In the matter of course, we eat the fruit, provided it has been made sufficiently attractive and palatable to us.

Too many of us are getting adept at this receiving without doing our part in creating. Too many of us are developing the attitude that it is up to others to do our thinking and producing for us. When by chance we do have to take part in production, we want sure-fire formulas, easy to follow and quick in results.

More tragic still is it that we carry this attitude into the more immaterial aspects of our personal lives, our success as individuals, our happiness, our mental and spiritual growth, and our human relations. We want easy, quick formulas for the achievement of these, and we want the formulas presented by our speakers and writers in *pablum* form, garnished to make it pleasant to the taste, and predigested to eliminate for us the effort of mastication and digestion.

Unfortunately, however, there are no quick and easy formulas for mental or spiritual growth. The way to competency is long and arduous. The road to happiness is a narrow one. The path to good human relations is through selflessness and discipline. And to whichever of these elevated peaks we wish to climb, we must do the traveling ourselves. There are no short cuts, no easy curves or grades, no magic tricks of the trade.

No one, for instance, can give us a formula for happiness and mass-produce it with a machine. Nor can they give us a simple recipe nor one in *pablum* form. This holds true also for human relations, for spiritual growth, or for simple business or worldly success. All these are the end-products of behavior which include honesty of purpose, personal detachment, diligent effort, trust, selfless action, compassion, and perseverance. No man nor jinni can be summoned to be or do these for us. In these we are strictly on our own, and there are no short cuts nor easy paths.

GETTING OFF THE LIMB

Some of our most valuable lessons we learn from the world of nature.

One of these is from the mother bird and her fledgling. In the middle summer of each year it is a repeated experience for him who observes nature to witness a mother bird taking her fledgling out on the limb and then shoving him off. She knows instinctively that her child must learn to use his wings if he is to play his part in the world of life and action. She knows, too, that in the wings of her offspring there lie potentially great strength, and agility, and power, but that control and mastery of these come only through the use of the wings.

So it is also with the human being. He, too, has wings; not one set of them, but a multitude. He has physical, spiritual, mental, and emotional wings, all inherently capable of high performance if he makes the effort to learn to use them. But he must throw himself off the limb, or he must be shoved off by someone else, perhaps his parents, his mate, or his boss. He can develop or progress only in proportion to how much he has learned to use his wings.

Parents and teachers have a great responsibility in this respect to the children in their care. By gently putting them on their own, by guiding them into making decisions, by permitting them to act independently, by making them do certain tasks and assume small responsibilities, they can help the child to use his wings. It is aiding him in growing into manhood and maturity. If, on the other hand, they do everything for him the child will remain a fledgling regardless of his age or physical growth.

The supervisor of employees or the business industrial executive has a real opportunity also to surround himself with more useful and valuable men and women. He must develop them by making them learn to use their own wings.

He puts people on their own. He gives them duties to perform, and responsibilities to assume. He forever shoves them off the limb, as it were, to help them develop new skills, and powers, and abilities. He expects awkward flights at first. He expects mistakes, and even some casualties. But he knows that the only way to develop ability to perform is through doing, and that for every casualty there will be ninety-nine who will come through with greater power and strength.

The individual, too, must constantly be shoving himself off the limb if he wishes to grow stronger, and more resourceful, and more useful. He will take on new duties and new obligations. He will take paths that he has not traveled before. He will, if necessary, put himself into spots where he must swim or sink. The odds are all in his favor that he will come through a stronger man with a richer life.

IS IT VITAL AND IMPORTANT?

—◆◆◆—

We believe it was Elbert Hubbard who coined the phrase: "Don't take life too serious. You'll never get out of it alive nohow."

It impressed us that there is a great deal of practical, common sense philosophy in these words.

No one would venture to deny the very great importance of taking life seriously, but there is such a thing as taking it *too* seriously. This is true especially of the myriad things that in the course of life arise to worry, annoy, and irritate us, but that are neither here nor there in importance in the total picture or outcome of our lives.

We allow ourselves to "stew" and fret about things so relatively insignificant that they do not merit a second consideration. We permit ourselves to become irritated and annoyed by things of such trivial nature that they deserve no more than a passing glance.

Worrying, "stewing," and being annoyed and irritated take time and consume precious energy. What is more is that these unpleasant states of mind linger on and are difficult to dislodge from our systems because they give us a false sense of satisfaction. They are often nothing more than manifestations of man's pouting because he did not get his way or because his ego has been bruised.

Taking life too seriously frequently bespeaks a puerile sense of values. In such cases, we magnify things out of their true proportions. Temporary financial difficulties; minor illness; accidental frustration of personal plans; inability to keep up with the Joneses; petty social blunders or slights; fancied preferences shown to others by our employers; slights to our ego; failure to close a sale or business deal; natural or human interferences with the getting of our own way; and hundreds of similar things are given the hue and color of catastrophic misfortunes.

It is said that one of the most distinguishing marks of the really educated or mature person is the ability to classify things as to their proper value. He separates the important from the unimportant; the temporary from the permanent; and reacts to each accordingly. Unlike his less mature fellow human being he devotes his efforts to that which has a total effect on his life, and treats lightly the innumerable daily happenings that are mere incidental annoyances and obstacles.

Yet it is these trivia that cost most of us our greatest concern. We make them the essence of our lives, rather than treat them as petty incidentals to be expected and disposed of as a matter of daily routine.

Thus we fret away our time and energy, and destroy for ourselves the full realization of our wonderful potentialities, simply because we take life too seriously. We do not distinguish between that which has lasting value and that which has little or no value; between that which is important and vital and that which is not.

INDIVIDUAL COMPETENCE TAKES TIME

This is an age of impatience and speed. Whatever we set out to do, we want to accomplish fast. We don't want to take time to make the journey. All we wish is to reach the goal.

We are impatient to get the job done. The manner in which it is done or the quality of the completed work is secondary in our thinking. What matters to us is that we get through with it.

We start out in our automobiles to make a journey whether it is to our work, to a friend's house, or to a distant city. The purpose is to get there and back. The enjoyment of the journey is of no importance to us.

This impatience is unfortunate in its effect on both the quality of our performance and upon the quantity and degree of our pleasures. Because of it, expert craftsmanship has become a rarity in both individual and mass productions. And as far as our daily pleasures are concerned, they are reduced to a minimum simply because we do not take the time to experience them.

The greatest evil that has come to us, however, because of this sense of hurry and its concomitant impatience, is that it has crept into our thinking about the development and fruition of ourselves. We have come to the point that we avoid making the effort to develop ourselves into competent beings, or taking the time to be seasoned into mature ones.

We want to spring into full manhood and its competence and rewards, without going through the growing pains of childhood, adolescence, and young adulthood. We want the wages of the expert without having so much as completed our apprenticeship. We demand the prestige of the executive without having disciplined and conditioned ourselves to accept the responsibilities that are inherent in his task.

What it all amounts to is that we want the rewards without first paying the price. And the price for human value is development and growth. This means work. It means the acquisition of knowledge and skill. It means the full assimilation of the great moral and spiritual principles. It means becoming mature physically, vocationally, morally, mentally, and spiritually. And above all things, it means *time* and *patience*.

Human fruition is a slow process. It cannot be hurried. It is the development of many individual forces, skills, and powers. And finally it is the slow integration of all of these into one living unit: the well-balanced, competent, disciplined, and mature individual.

WHAT IS THE PRICE?

There are a great many things that each of us would like to have in the daily course of his life.

A few of these are things that are needed to maintain our lives at a minimum standard. Many of the things we want, however, are to satisfy acquired or even imaginary needs, and are not strictly necessary. They are usually desirable, are good to have, and do add to the ease and graciousness and comfort of our lives.

The important consideration about obtaining these extras of life, however, is the price we have to pay for them. The question is what is their value to us in relationship to the human values we have to give up to obtain them. How often, for instance, must the father of a family weigh the value of a new car or gun, let us say, against the cost of other values to his family. If the purchase of the desired article means monthly anxiety to pay the installments; if it requires reduction of an already limited food budget; if it calls for depriving the family of needed clothing, or of desirable social, recreational, and educational activity, perhaps the price to be paid in total value is too high.

Other things we want in life are ambivalent in nature. In other words, they are the opposite of each other. To have one, we must give up the other at least to some degree. We cannot, for instance, be physically muscular and athletic in the highest degree and yet lead a life that is primarily scholarly and sedentary. We must be willing to sacrifice one for the other. In other words, if we want to stay at home, we must forego traveling abroad.

The important thing is that we have to pay a price for whatever we want. In everyday life it becomes a matter of balancing that which we gain against that which we lose. The important thing is to learn to recognize a price that is too high.

The matter of price, however, works in the opposite way, too. Sometimes the price is so low that we cannot afford not to pay it for the things we want. How often, for instance, will a few hours of extra work, or a short time spent on self-improvement each day provide us with the means to obtain the things we want? Does not every salesman know the dividends paid to him for a few extra hours of prospecting and of sales preparation? Can anyone question the high values that result from the low price paid in effort and time for daily mental, spiritual, and social development? Who can afford not to pay the price when he has to give so little to receive so much?

Full and satisfying living is to a large extent a matter of following the price rule. When is the price so high that I cannot afford to pay it; and when is it so low in relationship to values expected that I cannot afford not to pay it?

THE WILL TO SUCCEED

Success comes to us only through our will to succeed.

It is never an accident. It does not come as a gift of heaven. It cannot be bestowed on us by rich and influential friends and associates. It is true that they can give us the trappings that indicate it, and can sometimes help us attain it. The real thing, however, that is the substance of success, must be made by ourselves. It is the end product of our own efforts. It is the result of our will to succeed.

Men have this will, or they don't. They succeed or fail accordingly. They have it only, however, if they have a vision of something they wish to accomplish or to be. It is the dreams they have that make men wish to succeed.

All of us begin life with dreams, visions, and high hopes. Somehow or other, however, we lose these visions. But it is infinitely worse that we lose the ability to have them. It is with this loss of our power to dare to imagine and to vision with the freshness of youth, that we also lose our will to succeed. Without the dreams and the visions there are no goals to will to accomplish.

What happens when we lose the visions is simply illustrated by the dream common at sometime or other to most young boys of becoming policemen and cowboys. The reason that comparatively few of them give fruition to this dream is not their realization of the impracticability of a society in which all male members are policemen or cowboys. It is not their lack of necessary capacity or potential. It is rather that they out-grow the dream. In other words they lose it, and with it the will to accomplish it.

So is it true with us in adult life. It is not lack of capacity, for instance, that keeps us from fruition. It is rather that we have no concrete dreams or visions that we want badly enough to actualize to give us the will to succeed.

But without this will we are stalemated. We ride along with the stream of life hoping vaguely for greater things, but doing little or nothing to achieve them. We do not take active charge of things to direct them towards the achievement of our personal goals. We live rather in a hazy expectation or hope that something will happen that will improve our circumstances and conditions.

The individual, however, who has the will to succeed takes charge of his success. He knows what he wants and he plans the steps by which to achieve it. He directs and bends the force of his life to the attainment of his goals. He does not expect fate to throw success in his lap, nor does he rely on other people to give it to him. He knows what he wants, and he regulates his daily actions to attain it. He succeeds because he has the will to succeed.

THE ACID TEST OF SUCCESS

No concept of success can be divorced from peace of mind.

Success is more than technological excellence, wealth, power, and fame. These are mere accomplishments or the result of accomplishments.

Success has an added ingredient that is indispensable to it. It contains a subjective factor which might be described as the individual's coming to terms with himself and his life through what he is and does. It is a matter of establishing a relationship with life that is both materially and spiritually satisfying.

Accomplishment is among the media we use to establish this relationship. But unless our accomplishments give meaning and significance to our lives; unless they give us a sense of self-fulfillment; unless in their totality they give us peace of mind, they cannot be considered as being synonymous with real success.

Peace of mind comes to us only when our ways of living and our accomplishments are in harmony with our deeper inner purposes; and then only if our purposes and our methods of accomplishing them are in harmony with the best interests of our fellow men.

No accomplishment or way of life, for instance, will give us peace of mind if it is purely selfish or self-directed. It is not easy to explain why this is true, but the experiences of mankind have verified it. If this is not sufficient proof, we need but look into our own hearts. The nature of the human being is manifestly such that man cannot get the sense of self-fulfillment, with its consequent peace of mind, out of ends that are solely self-directed.

Nor can he get peace of mind out of methods of accomplishing these purposes that are out of harmony with the fundamental virtues that mankind accepts as the cardinal ones in all human inter-relationships.

Unjust acts, as an example, are barbarities that are cankerous to peace of mind. Nearly as destructive are acts bereft of compassion. Close to these are acts and relationships of arrogance. And probably not far removed from these corrosive cardinal acts, are our many minor daily human relationships in which we use our Divinely designed hands as if they were the paws of monkeys.

Being successful in the real sense is more than a matter of objective accomplishment. Indispensable to it is a subjective element, namely, that these accomplishments have fulfilled the deeper inner purposes of our hearts: always without needlessly interfering with our fellow men or other living creatures in the fulfillment of their inner purposes; and, whenever possible, in a manner that will help them in the full realization of their lives.

The acid test of real success, regardless of the magnitude of our objective accomplishments, is, "Has it given us peace of mind?"

GIVE, AND IT SHALL BE GIVEN YOU!

From times ancient as the human race, wise men have recognized the significance of the relationship of giving and of receiving.

It was, however, the great Teacher, Jesus, who first declared it as a fundamental law of life—a law which in the spiritual aspects of living is as certain in its working, and as inexorable, as is the law of gravitation in the physical nature of things.

"Give, and it shall be given unto you—good measure, pressed down, and shaken together, and running over shall men give unto your bosom. For with the same measure that you mete withal it shall be measured to you again . . ."

It is a simple, but vital principle of living. And it is a specific promise. It is an assurance of a return in overflowing measure—"good measure, pressed down, and shaken together, and running over."

Men who have believed in it and have tried it have found it unfailing. Personal, spiritual, and industrial empires have been built on the inevitable working of this great law.

It is the giving to and sharing with others of ourselves and of what we have. Especially is it the giving of ourselves in the daily relationships of life—the personal giving of that which costs us nothing: sympathy, understanding, helpfulness, consideration, friendliness.

St. Francis of Assisi stated it beautifully in his immortal Prayer:—

Grant that I may not so much
Seek to be consoled as to console;
To be understood as to understand;
To be loved as to love.

For it is in giving that we receive!

Philosophers and psychologists have pronounced it a basic, inherited human need. If we wish, they say, our own lives to be full and happy ones, we must first learn to give of ourselves to others in helpfulness and service.

It is a basic law of life!

THE PRICELESS AND IRREPLACEABLE TODAY

The only day of any importance in our lives is today.

To elevate its quality is, according to Henry Thoreau, the highest of arts.

To do so is to shape the very nature and quality of our lives. For it is today that we live. It is not tomorrow. Some of us are presumptuous enough to believe that the future belongs to us, but the real truth is that only today is ours, and that if we do not live today we miss life with all its potential accomplishment and happiness.

The universal and tragic truth of missing life because we do not live it today was ably expressed by the eminent Blaise Pascal in the seventeenth century when he stated that because we hope to live, we never do so; and that because we are always preparing to be happy, it is inevitable that we will never be so.

It is, then, because we are procrastinators or "putter-offers" of life that we live such negative and unchallenging lives. We do not allow ourselves to be and do our best. We reserve this for another more propitious day.

Perpetually to us, tomorrow looks more favorable, better to work, to give, to love: to be our best and finest selves. In our thinking, always the tomorrow is more advantageously free from the frustrations and obstacles that beset us today.

The essential fact we forget, namely, that tomorrow is the future, and that only today is life. Somehow or other the vital point escapes us that to assure a worth-while and happy life we must live our hopes, our dreams, and our ideals today. It is this day that is the only one of importance—today—not a spent yesterday, nor an anticipated tomorrow.

In view of this it is apparent that there are few things so tragic as letting a day slip by without living it as we ultimately hope to live. Today is the most priceless possession we have. It is also an irreplaceable one. If we waste it or lose it, we have been foolishly prodigal, indeed. No good resolutions nor repentance can merit for us the chance to live it again. It is eternally lost.

THE FALLACY OF ENVIOUSLY COMPETING

- -<del>◦◖◗◦</del>-

All of us could have richer lives if we made a little more effort to try to help one another satisfy the human hungers that are essentially part of every man, woman, and child.

For some reason or other we have not learned well the wisdom of this simplest and most obvious of all lessons of good living. For some strange reason, rather than be helpful to one another, we are in envious competition with our fellow human beings. It seems as if we lived in constant fear that the other person might get more out of life than we are getting.

In our struggle with one another for material possessions, for recognition, for love, and for status, we act as if the Creator of the universe had severely limited the quantity of the things needed by man for the maintenance and enrichment of his life. To our limited finite minds, unlimited supply is inconceivable. As a result, we act as if we had to scramble for the satisfaction of our human needs lest the supply be exhausted before we had our needed take.

To rid ourselves of this urge to enviously compete with others, we need a more realistic point of view. We need to understand if every human being of the past, the present, and the future surfeited himself with an abundance of all things tangible and intangible, that the universal supply would be less depleted than an ocean from which a single drop of water has been taken.

We need to understand that we do not enviously have to compete with one another for our share of the necessities and comforts of life, and that such competing is a fallacy because of which men often defeat themselves. By competing in place of cooperating and of helping one another, we cut ourselves off from the main supply line to unlimited abundance.

Since most of the essential and priceless things we need for our well-being and happiness, such as being important, having status, belonging, being needed, and being loved can come to us only through our fellow human beings, it is necessarily these human beings who are our main line of supply.

To compete with them is to compete with ourselves. To withhold from them is to withhold from ourselves. To take from them what they need for abundant lives, is to deplete the supply which they have available for us and upon which we must feed for our abundance.

Enviously to compete is to be blindly foolish. The wiser course is to help others enrich their lives. Then the more they will have to return to us to enrich ours.

RESOLVING OUR PROBLEMS

All of us have our difficulties and problems.

Some of these problems are grievous ones; others are mere annoyances. Over a period of a lifetime their extent and severity is probably about the same for most of us. If we traded for those of another human being, it would probably be a nearly even swap.

In terms of living, this means that problems are a common lot, and as such we ought to expect them, accept them as more or less natural, and meet them objectively in our efforts to solve them.

Like hunger or thirst, problems give us displeasure and thus egg us on to do something about them. They create tensions that spur us into action. They are stimuli to which we respond in one way or another, either subjectively through emotion or objectively through action.

No one of us would think of resolving the problems of hunger and thirst with emotional feeding. We solve them by taking food and drink. We meet them objectively through action.

Strangely, however, to most of the problems of life we tend to react emotionally. We meet them subjectively as if they could be solved through worry and anxiety. In place of resorting to planned action in our conquest of them, we stew emotionally about them. We try to feed them, not with the appropriate food and drink, but rather with fear, worry, and anxiety. In place of trying to resolve them through action, we mope about them in self-pity.

It is admitted that there are a few problems that cannot be solved. There are also a few of which the solution depends almost entirely on agencies outside of ourselves. The overwhelming majority of our problems, however, are within our control and can be solved by us if we set out earnestly to seek a way.

Man is not like a member of a socialized insect colony. He need not become lost and helpless when he is diverted by obstacles and problems from his accustomed way of life. His way of living is not blindly instinctual as is that of the bee or ant. His life is, on the other hand, subject to his personal control, and as a rational creature he has the capacity to figure out ways and means to deal with the hinderances and obstacles that threaten his way of living.

But he must plan and he must act. He must take charge of the problems that obstruct his way. The emotions of fear, worry, and anxiety, although they are initial spurs to action, ultimately become mere escapes from it. They solve nothing. It is, thus, what man does about his problems, not how he reacts to them emotionally, that is the thing that counts in resolving them.

NEED FOR THE OLD-FASHIONED ROCKING CHAIR

One of our most critical needs in America today is the return to our living rooms of at least one, and preferably two or three old-fashioned rocking chairs.

We need time to sit and rock at leisure; to accept and enjoy life as it is. We need time, too, to reflect, to evaluate, and to think out clearly just what it is we want from the feverish chase that has become synonymous with living.

As it is now, we are in a perpetual turmoil. We spend our days and nights in the circular pursuit of our tails; and the more we chase, the more feverish the pursuit becomes and the more frustrating the fruitless pursuit.

In the light of this maddening tension and strife for the things that never seem to satisfy our real wants and longings, it is not surprising to the physician, the psychologist, the psychiatrist, or the priest that we, as a nation, have to consume millions of pounds of aspirin each year to keep our heads from splitting. Nor is it surprising to them that we need millions of sleeping tablets each night to calm our feverish minds and our racking emotion. Nor is it particularly mysterious to them that one out of twelve of us Americans at some time or another in his lifetime must seek psychiatric help; and that one of us every twenty-four minutes of the day and night finds escape through suicide.

Nor is it an enigma to the philosophers that in spite of all of our material comforts and riches, so few of us find even a fair semblance of contentment and peace of mind. Their explanation is simple, namely, that there are certain essential things that men live by, but that men obtain these neither through feverish pursuit, nor by the chase after will-o'-the-wisps.

Since we are largely guilty of both of these defeating activities, perhaps the old-fashioned rocking chair would tend to set us right again. Sitting and rocking for a spell each day would help break the tension of the pursuit. Eventually it would help quiet our nerves and clear our minds sufficiently to enable us to see life in terms of its genuine values and in a much truer perspective.

It is unfortunate that we have become so involved in the pursuit of that for which we strive, that we have neither the time nor the composure to examine the validity of our objectives. We spend our lives trying to attain them, but without first relating them to human happiness and well-being. We strive for them as blindly as we do feverishly, not knowing if they are essential values or mere phantoms.

Although an hour or two each day in an old-fashioned rocking chair would by no means be a cure for all our ills, it would, nevertheless, calm us down. The least it would do in the long run is to help keep us from the psychiatric couch. It would detach us for awhile from the feverish struggle, and enable us to see life impartially and objectively from the side lines with a better view of what is important to the play, what is merely incidental, and also what is defeating and destructive. Last, but not least, it would give us enough time with ourselves to discover the richness of our blessings, and to find the wells of joy and contentment that are within our own hearts.

GROW WE MUST

If a human being wishes to maintain his present status, or if he wishes to advance above it, he must continue to grow both as a person and as a doer of things.

There is no such thing as a static point in human development. This means if a person stops growing, he begins to deteriorate. He has reached the zenith of his accomplishments, and has started to go downward as far as the fruition of himself and his life is concerned. In other words, he's through. He is done for.

The human scene is crowded with such individuals who have gone as far as they are going, and who are gradually, almost imperceptibly, losing the status they have attained, simply because they are not doing anything to further personal or vocational growth.

We find them in the offices, in the assembly lines, and in the homes. We find them in positions high and low. Many of them have the potentialities greatly to better themselves. And it is safe to say that none of them have developed their powers to the fullest. All of them could go further if they put in the effort that nurtures continued growth.

It would be difficult to conceive a circumstance in which a human being could find no ways to additional personal growth. If there were no other way, he could continue to grow through the more complete assimilation of that which he already knows or has experienced.

Stoppage of growth is usually the result of personal factors. It is probable that in many cases it is brought about and tolerated by an individual because he thinks and feels that he "knows it all, and that no further growth is necessary or even possible." Or it could be the result of a lack of realization on his part that growth has stopped. Or it could be, and we suspect that this is the most prevalent reason, that the individual is unwilling to make the effort required.

It is seldom, if ever, brought about because of the lack of opportunity. The avenues or means to growth are too numerous to make plausible such an excuse. We can continue to grow in any one, or in any combinations of many ways, and most of these are available in some degree to every individual.

For instance, we grow by doing things we have never done before; also by assuming added responsibilities. We grow by association with those of greater experience, and by making available to ourselves the oral and written expressions of the specialist. We grow by reading and studying according to a purpose. And, finally, we grow by quiet periods of thought and meditation in which we assimilate our daily experiences and our newly acquired knowledge.

But grow we must, and we have to do it through our own efforts. No one outside of ourselves can do it for us. To fail to do so means a gradual decline into passivity and its consequent mediocrity.

NO FREE BUGGY RIDES

Many sincere men are alarmed today about the increasing numbers of people who are looking for free buggy rides through life.

We have these people in homes, in business institutions, in communities, and in practically every collective activity of life. They are the free-riders who live off the labors of others. They are the men and women who take the benefits of group activity, but who accept little or no responsibility for doing their share in creating the benefits they consume. In the world of nature we would call them parasites.

It is difficult to understand how men and women can delude themselves into adopting as a way of life such a concept of social irresponsibility. The primordial command to mankind was that it shall earn its bread by the sweat of its brow. Equally primordial is the elementary principle of justice that no one has taken away from him that which is rightfully his. The individual who lives off the labors of others violates both.

Any reasonably mature human being, of course, accepts the fact that the young, the physically sick, the mentally incompetent, the deeply bereaved, and the senile have a right to share fully in the labors of those of productive capacity. On the other hand, all just and socially responsible men, however, challenge the right of the free-rider. Fairness and justice demand that in a society of men, small or large, the adult, the physically strong and the mentally healthy contribute in proportion to what they receive from the socialized effort. Any form of partially or totally "free-riding along" on the efforts of others is a perversion and an evil.

If men realized the lack of justice of thus living off the efforts of others, there would probably be much less of it. To elevate the plane of living of a family or to run a business successfully requires the full effort of each and every member or employee. To have someone not contribute his share in proportion to the benefits that he takes from it, either places an extra load on others or deprives others of the full benefits of their labors. No group that has within it individuals who will not do their share can operate for the maximum benefits of all concerned.

Free buggy riders drain away the benefits earned for the group by its productive workers.

DOING IT NOW

There is no instant of time so favorable to us as is the present one.

The past is history. The future is unborn. To live in either is to dwell in a dreamland of memory or of fantasy.

The only reality of time is the present moment. It is within it that we must make of our lives what we wish them to be. So is it also within it that we must be what we hope to become.

To be and to do it now; that is the secret to successful and purposive living. To put it off till tomorrow is the way to inactivity and ultimate nonrealization.

What we intend to be or do tomorrow does not count at the present moment. It does not affect the actual quality of our lives an iota. Conversely, however, the present moment is the embryo of tomorrow. The caliber of our today foreshadows the caliber of any tomorrow that may be given us.

It is only what we think, say, and do at this moment that is our life and that makes it one of low or high quality. The only effective moment is now. To treat it in any other way is merely an attempt to escape from reality.

In the thinking of most of us human beings, life lies in the future. It is in the days ahead when circumstances are more opportune that we plan to live fully and effectively. The present to us seldom seems propitious for the exercise of our potentially highest qualities and virtues, or for the application of our best efforts.

We have a tendency to put off living until some other day in the long future before us. We put off until tomorrow the efforts necessary to improve our work, or the changes required to better our personal selves. We resist both effort and change in the full expectation that some day, miraculously, we will do the things that will make for us a full life.

It is also tomorrow that we will change our work habits to make us more effective in our jobs. It is tomorrow that we will do the tasks at hand, one by one as they arise, skillfully and completely. So is it, too, tomorrow that we will set about developing the internal graces that are character, and the external traits and habits that translate these graces into outward actions in relationships with our fellow men.

But the point is that life is now, and that it consists of the thoughts and actions of the moment. The changes for the better that we are going to make on a more favorable tomorrow are ghostly delusions. Tomorrow is merely an unborn today that will be lived by us according to the pattern wrought by our thoughts and actions on the today that has become a yesterday.

What we wish to be or to do tomorrow, we must then be and do now. It is the only certain way to live fully and effectively—or to live at all.

EACH DAY ONE OF THANKSGIVING

If we were a bit more grateful for the things we have, we would be considerably less unhappy about those that we do not have.

Life is a bounteous giver, but since its gifts are freely bestowed and are so frequently of the nature of a bequest to us, we accept them as a matter of fact and with no sense of recognition or of obligation.

The blunt truth is that the greater number of the things that contribute most to our well-being and happiness are ones to which we have no right by way of effort or earning. We inherit them from our Creator and from the men who have lived before us or are living with us.

The earth, which is our dwelling place, and by the fruits of which we live, is a divine gift. So are our beautifully designed bodies; our minds; our free wills; our potential skills; our abilities to feel nobly, to love, to aspire, and to live courageously and justly.

The culture and civilization into which we are born, on the other hand, were inherited from the men who preceded us. They are precious gifts made possible through the toils and sufferings of countless human beings over a period of thousands of years.

To these inheritances must be added the rich contributions made to us by our parents, friends, and other contemporary benefactors. Our fine homes, our industrial pre-eminence, our medical and other scientific advances are not accidental. They are rather the results of the endeavors of those of our contemporary fellow men who are devoting themselves to the continued betterment of the life of man. We, however, are the receivers of these blessings, not the creators or givers of them.

When we weigh in the balance what we have received and what we have given, we find an unlimited disproportion. So, too, is it with what has been bestowed on us and what we have earned through our own efforts.

The tendency of too many of us, however, is that we take the blessings for granted. We show little evidence of being grateful for them. In place of an attitude of thanksgiving, we have one of further demand. We literally make ourselves unhappy by wanting more and more, and usually of the things that are neither here nor there of essential importance to our well-being and our happiness.

Perhaps man would be infinitely happier and more content if he spent less time on his knees begging for what he thinks he needs and wants, and more time thanking his God and the race of man for the blessings he has received gratuitously.

If happiness can be defined, we doubt if there is a better definition of it than living in a state of gratefulness and appreciation. Of this we are certain, namely, that all of us would enjoy fuller, richer, and more rewarding lives if we made of every day of the year, a Day of Thanksgiving.

IT'S THE FIRST DOWNS THAT COUNT

---◄◉►---

Every good football player knows that the purpose of a play is to make a first down. It is not the making of a touchdown. Getting the ball behind the final goal line takes care of itself if enough consecutive first downs are made.

As the football player, so does the skilled player in the game of life know that the trick to success is the making of first downs. To him the first down, or the immediate goal of his efforts, is the day at hand. The plays or the tries he makes to reach that goal are the daily situations and tasks of which he is a part, and to which he must respond in one way or another.

He knows, too, that touchdowns are rarely made through spectacular passes or long field runs. They are rather the inevitable result of a cumulation of successive days well lived and effectively achieved.

To assure the success of each day is, therefore, the goal with which he is concerned. To reach it he concentrates his fullest efforts on every opportunity given him "to carry the ball." He accepts the challenge of each situation and task and makes the most of it. It is in this concentration that there lies his best assurance of succeeding often enough to make each day a first down. And it follows that in the game of life as in that of football, the achievement of the ultimate goal of life is a natural consequence of "first downs" or individual days successfully completed.

No person, regardless of his skill or experience, can, of course, move forward on every try he makes. There are times when the forces blocking his forward movement are insurmountable. There are other times when he does not have the skill to cope with the situation at hand. Many times he is not up to par in his performance. Sometimes he fumbles and needs temporarily to go on the defensive. Although these ineffective tries set him back for the moment, they rarely keep him from ultimate success. It is the cumulative results of his tries that count, and although he may fail in some attempts he does not thereby forfeit his chances of ultimate victory.

The thing that counts in the achievement of the ultimate goal of his life is the over-all pattern of day-after-day performance. The winning or losing factor is a matter of what he does with average consistency. If he devotes his full effort to the successful execution of each task or opportunity to make of every day a measured unit of success, the reaching of the ultimate purpose of his life is inevitable. If, on the other hand, he is indifferent in the execution of his daily tasks, or applies himself to them with faint-hearted and undisciplined effort, he is with near certainty doomed to failure. This is true also if he lives in the vague hope of making a spectacular across-the-field run to his goal.

Consistently to make first downs is truly the secret to effective living.

THE OLD AND THE NEW

The past is a thing of the past. Neither we nor God can change its course. Its final chapter has been written. We had best forget it.

To brood in regret over what it might have been, or to look back with remorse over our shortcomings and failures in the use of it is childish. It serves no purpose except to misdirect and consume the energy that might be applied to the building of a better future.

Fortunately or unfortunately, of course, as the individual case may be, the past cannot be obliterated from our present or our future. Its infinite variety of experiences such as its successes and failures, its moments of elevation and degradation, its noble and base thoughts and acts—all have been recorded in our personality and character.

The person we are now is a composite of these experiences of our past. No experience, be it ever so small or so large, is lost. It is there, and will to some degree or extent have to be reckoned with in the determination of the conduct of the future.

We can, however, enhance the value of the good experiences, and lessen the effect of the negative ones, through the determined effort to assure a preponderance of wholesome and elevating experiences in the present and in the future.

In other words, the success of the present and of the future can be assured through the daily application of the lessons we have learned from the past. It is a matter of doing what experience has taught us leads to successful and happy living, and of avoiding that which dooms us to frustration and failure.

Man himself is largely the shaper of his own life. He is the sculptor who molds its form. He is the artist who creates of it a masterpiece if he wills. He creates of it a masterpiece, but not by living in regrets for past mistakes and inactivities. He does it rather through a life of positive action for the good. He takes himself as he is, eliminates his weaknesses, and builds up his strengths. He learns the rules of success and happiness and abides by them. He determines to do only that which is right, and follows the course with confidence and assurance. For the rest, he places himself "under the feathers of God, and knows that under His wing he can trust."

Ultimately, then, it matters little what the past has been. The future is ours if we will but take it and shape it into the successful and prosperous one we want it to be.

THE PATTERN IS THE THING

Give a seamstress the directions of how you wish a new dress made, and the odds are that she will come up with a garment that is unlike the one you had in mind. It will make little difference how specific and complete your directions are.

Give to her, on the other hand, a pattern to follow, and the odds are equally great that she will deliver to you the garment of your specifications.

So is it, too, in the creating and shaping of human personalities by the men and women who have the responsibilities of guidance and of leadership. Directions and precepts are important, but their effectiveness depends on the pattern that accompanies them. It is the pattern that counts. Directions are mere words; the pattern is the words embodied. Words are heard; patterns are seen. Patterns give direction by example. They are, too, the living proof that the words have validity and substance.

Whether it is the father or mother in a family; the magistrate in a community; the priest in his parish; the teacher in the classroom; or the executive in business or industrial leadership; it is the pattern he sets that will be followed and that will shape the people under him. It is the pattern his people will emulate, not the preachings that flow from his mouth.

If we would influence to good the lives of others we must give them ourselves as a pattern. If we wish them to be that which we would like them to be, we must first become it ourselves. We must be the pattern and the proof. The most con-

106

vincingly effective sermon is to be an example, and the easiest pattern for men and women to follow is the one of ourselves that we set before them.

The fledgling bird imitates the song of the mother bird on the tree top. It needs no verbal direction, nor proof of the quality of the tune. So, too, men follow the pattern set by their parents, prophets, magistrates, and other leaders, and they accept as worthy patterns of behavior whatever values are distinctive in the ways of life that are thus set before them.

Men and women become what their leaders are; not what they pretend to be, not what they preach, but what they prove themselves to be in the small and large relationships of life irrespective of personal expediency.

Without the pattern the words are bare. It is the pattern that is the thing.

GOOD INTENTIONS ARE NOT ENOUGH

It is said that a merciful heaven rewards good intentions.

Unfortunately, life in terms of successful accomplishment does not pay off on that basis.

In our everyday living we must live according to the principles of right living and success, or we pay the price in impotency.

Good intentions in the accomplishment of objectives do not count by themselves. Ignorance of the principles of success; inadequate skill; lack of industry; or such mitigating factors as poor environment or lack of opportunity are not overlooked or pardoned. They are not accepted as excuses. We overcome these and rise above them or fail correspondingly in performance.

Success is not an accident. Nor is it a magical thing reserved for a favored few. It is rather an inevitable result of a prescribed way of thinking and acting. Although it is never alike for any two individuals, the methods of attaining it are alike for all men. Success for any individual human being is the using of his own unique talents and potentialities according to known ways of making them most effective.

Among the more fundamental of the known ways of effectively using his talents is that he must first decide what objective use he wants to make of them. Energies and abilities must be directed toward a definite end or goal. Man must know specifically what he wants to accomplish. Life does not pay off on the basis of the diffusion and dissipation of talents and energies.

A second known way is that objectives are more likely reached if man plans the route he will follow to attain them. Here again life does not compensate for detours or for getting "lost in the woods." It counts only the distance man travels on the shortest and most direct path to the goal.

A third known way is that he must get into action. He must put in the effort required. Man cannot grasp a star if he does not reach for it. Neither will he get food for his table, nor shelter for his family, nor knowledge and skill in the exercise of his talents by merely visualizing them or wishing for them. The only manna that life rains down on him is that which he has merited and produced through his physical and mental efforts.

And closely related to this third way is a fourth one, namely, that he persevere in his efforts towards reaching the desired goal. It is commonly referred to as "stick-to-itiveness." Many men fail not because they do not work hard enough but because they do not do so long enough. The history of successful accomplishment is one of trying just once more in the face of repeated failures.

THE DIRECT ROUTE TO FAILURE

There is no factor or element in life that brings about failure more directly and surely than a lack of integrity.

Integrity implies wholeness and soundness of living. It means that we live in a manner that protects and furthers the best interests of ourselves and of our fellow human beings.

Lack of integrity, then, suggests that our actions are such as would be harmful to the welfare and rights of either ourselves or of our neighbors. It means that we are in violation of the Moral Law ordained by God as a way of life that will assure well-being and the highest possible development to all human beings regardless of birth, or of financial or social status.

Whenever we do anything that needlessly hurts one of our fellows, or that infringes on his rights, we are lacking in integrity. We are committing an act that is harmful to us and that precipitates our failure both because it makes other people afraid of us and because it is a violation of the rules of life.

We cannot hurt others physically, financially, morally, spiritually, or any other way without inviting failure. To keep on doing such acts continuously makes failure inevitable.

When we deprive or take away from someone that which is rightfully his, we are lacking in integrity.

When we interfere with another's exercise of his natural rights to survive, to develop himself, and to attain happiness and success, we are lacking in integrity.

When we selfishly keep from another his rightful share of

tangible goods, or of intangible satisfactions, we are lacking in integrity.

When we promise to another values that actually do not exist in the commodity or service that we are selling him, we are lacking in integrity.

When we fail to pay a fair wage, give an earned promotion, or neglect to give an employee the necessary training to develop his talents and potential abilities, we are lacking in integrity.

When we fail to cooperate with other individuals or other departments towards the accomplishment of the common purpose or objective of an organization, we are hurting all members of that organization, and, consequently, we are lacking in integrity.

When we spread harmful gossip or insinuations about others, whether factual or fictional, we are lacking in integrity.

The penalty for lack of integrity is failure both in our jobs and in our lives. It is integrity which is the indispensable foundation of all human activities. Without it men could not live together in any satisfying way. Without it there is no safety, no trust, no security, and no honor in our relationship with each other.

THE THREE DIMENSIONS OF LIFE

One of our famous Americans of the past century, Phillips Brooks, taught that the life of man contained three dimensions. Mr. Brooks believed that if we wished to live to our fullest capacity, we must develop in all three of these dimensions, which he called "the length, the breadth, and the height of life."

We believe that the teachings of this renowned divine contains a great deal of wisdom, and that it can be of real help to us in obtaining from our lives the contentment, the success, and the happiness for which each of us strives.

By the "length" of life, he does not have reference to the number of years of its duration. He refers rather to that aspect of life which has to do with our concern about ourselves, our material needs, our ambitions, our hopes and dreams, and all the other things that we need or desire for ourselves personally.

And I think we will all agree that our first concern is ourselves, or that this dimension of "length" is of primary importance to us.

It is a basic human instinct to wish to survive and preserve ourselves. It is also a part of our nature to take care of ourselves first, and to strive not only for the minimum needs of survival, but also for the added things that we as individuals want for the expansion of our personal lives.

It is normal then, and right, and wise that we in the development of this first dimension of our lives, do the things that will better our individual status. It is a proper activity to seek greater earning power, better jobs, higher standards of living, greater social prestige, and the many other things that enhance our personal lives.

But this is only one dimension. He who concerns himself with the "length" only, and who works solely for that which satisfies only himself, will lead a very thin and tenuous life. Man must go beyond himself. He must reach outward to others. This is the second dimension, namely "breadth." If he wants his life to be otherwise than meaningless and shallow; if he wants contentment and happiness, he must, too, live for others. He must reach outwardly, away from himself, into "breadth" of life.

Brooks adds the dimension of "height," which is the reaching upward to a Being who is greater than we are. Man needs an anchor. He needs something to fasten himself onto. By nature he is limited, and feels insecure. He needs, therefore, to anchor onto that which is safe by being unlimited in power, and strength, and love. Only God is that, hence man's need to reach upward.

It is only, then, when man has developed in "length, and breadth, and height," that he has completed the substance of his life; for he has become dimensionally whole and sound.

THE RIGHT TO EARN YOUR SHARE

Many of us are concerned today with the great number of adult and able individuals who are prepared to accept the good things and privileges of life without contributing their full share of effort to deserve or create these things.

We are seriously alarmed by the many in the work and social group who expect from life its riches, comforts, and honors, not as a reward of their individual efforts, but as something they have coming to them as a right.

We are disturbed by this philosophy of receiving the remunerations of labor, without performing the labor; of getting the blessings, without making the sacrifices; of taking the credit of full effort, but doing only enough to get by; of demanding the fruit, without the sweat and toil of producing it.

We know of no justification in the scheme of life for the right of capable men and women to share in the benefits of group effort or production, unless they have made their full contribution to the creation of those benefits. We believe that the right to share is contingent on the doing of one's part in the creation of something. We believe that a right is not innate, but that it is acquired and earned; and that no one has a right to expect to share in anything unless he has done his full part in earning it.

The attitude of having something coming as a natural right from the social or work group, without having made an equal contribution to that group is indeed a strange one. Each of us is an individual charged with the responsibility of his own personal maintenance and development. It is true that he has potential rights from the group and from life. These, however, he can bring into fruition only through the acceptance and performance of certain obligations.

He has a right, for instance, to the means of a living, provided he earns them through the efforts of his hands, his head, or his heart.

He is entitled, too, to certain privileges provided he assumes the responsibilities that earn for him such privileges.

He has a right to increased wages and a higher standard of living, if he has made himself more useful and profitable to his employer or customer. He has a right to be considered for promotion to supervision, if he has developed in himself the necessary qualities of leadership. He has the privilege of being trusted to control and direct his own time and work, provided he has demonstrated his dependability. He is entitled to the privilege of being a husband, and father, and head of a family, when he has developed the necessary maturity to be responsible for the obligations of that high stewardship.

But at no time does the social or work group owe him these benefits and rights unless he is earning them, and is doing his share in making the same benefits available to the other members. He is not intended to be a parasite. He is a full participating member of the group who gives his part so he may have the right to share in the efforts and contributions of the whole.

We believe the only innate or acquired right that an individual, able of body and mind, and under normal circumstances, has to the benefits of group effort is that he receive in proportion to that which he gives. It should be no more and no less. He has a right to earn his share.

TAKING THINGS FOR GRANTED

An outstanding industrial psychologist has said that the Eleventh Commandment should be, "Thou shall not take thy fellow human being for granted."

We would like to venture to add an equally important Twelfth Commandment, namely, "Thou shall not take for granted the things of thy everyday life."

It is this matter of accepting the things that we live by as if they were our natural right that makes us lose appreciation of the infinite blessings that are the very fabric of our existence. We take for granted that which has become a part of the daily routine of our lives, never thinking that these are a heritage that has been made possible through the sacrifices of our forebearers, and through the beneficence of a Divine Providence.

It is so easy to take for granted the food we eat; the comforts and conveniences of our homes; our health and that of our loved ones; our high standards of living; the warmth that saves us from the winter's cold; the right to own the products of our labor; the freedom to move about, to live, to work, and to worship as we please.

It is also just as easy and natural for us to forget that these were not always the ways of life for mankind, and that, even today, millions of our fellow human beings have never tasted these blessings which to us are a matter of routine.

How many of us, for instance, ever think that for every one of us who has plentifulness of food, there is another human being somewhere in the world who is famished with hunger; that for every healthy and happy child, there is another crippled, and ill, and brought up in poverty and ignorance; that for every man, woman, and child who can raise his heart in worship to his God as he pleases, there is another one who can do so only under the threats of punishment, ostracism, or perhaps even of death?

Perhaps each day of our life should be a day of thanksgiving to keep alive in our hearts a sense of appreciation for the many blessings we have. I am certain of this, that if we were to quit taking things for granted, life would take on an entirely different meaning to us. Each day would be one of inspiration and challenge to continue to earn and safeguard the precious things that are ours. Each day, too, would be one of greater contentment and happiness, for are not these two the children of a heart filled with gratitude and appreciation?

OUR BASIC NEEDS

Our body has certain basic requirements which must be supplied to it if we wish it to function in a healthy manner.

But what is true of the body also applies to the whole human being, who in addition to the physical, has mental, emotional, spiritual, and social constituents. This whole being, therefore, too, has basic needs which must be fulfilled if he is to be a healthy and integrated person.

If one were, for instance, to keep proteins from one's food diet permanently, the body would become ill, simply because proteins are a basic requirement of the physical machine. It must have this food to run smoothly and efficiently, possibly even to survive.

So it is with the entire human person. Withhold from him for an extended period of time one of the things that he basically needs, and he becomes ill, although unfortunately in most cases he is unaware of it. The symptoms which develop, such as lack of buoyant happiness, lack of enthusiasm, lack of serenity and purpose, absence of interest and vitality, presence of ill humor, boredom, depression, fatigue, and hosts of others, he looks upon as being natural. Yet actually they are to the whole being, what high temperature is to the body. They are warning signals that something is not well with the functioning of the person, or with his way of life.

Fortunately, we have only a few basic, inherited needs. But they are vital, and unless there is a reasonably balanced satisfaction of all of them, our lives become blighted.

Dr. Thorpe, a great psychologist, believes there are only three such needs—satisfaction of physical stresses, recognition, and service.

Dr. Bell, eminent educator, scholar and theologian, believes there are only two—love and craftsmanship.

Many of the greatest teachers and prophets have stressed a fifth need, faith—belief in ourselves and in the great things we are capable of doing.

Accepting these five as fundamental needs, our greatest concern in life is to see that all of them are reasonably well cared for. It does not do, for instance, to satisfy four and neglect one. It is a fivesome, all demanding attention.

Satisfaction of physical needs or stresses, recognition, service or love, craftsmanship, and faith—these are the needs that we must satisfy in our day-by-day living. To neglect any one or more of them throws the human person and his life out of balance. It destroys the equilibrium of his nature. To satisfy them all, reasonably and proportionately, on the other hand, means health, happiness, peace of mind and of heart.

THE THREE SYSTEMS OF HABITS

In the development of human personality, we are particularly concerned with the habits and traits of the individual.

We human beings throughout our life development acquire hundreds, and perhaps thousands, of different habits of thinking and feeling, and acting. Some of these are acquired consciously others unconsciously. Their sum total, however, gives us the particular personality that makes us distinctively ourselves, and that determines our relationship to other people.

Good personality is made up of habits that make people respond to us favorably. Poor personality means the presence of some traits that bring about unfavorable response.

Our job, then, if we wish to get along well with people is to develop a pattern of desirable personality traits, with an exclusion of the traits that bring about an unfavorable reaction.

To do this, we are concerned with three systems of habits which include in them all automatic actions or responses. These systems of habits are those of appearance, talk, and action.

The first reaction of human beings is naturally to what they see when they look at us. It is a first impression, and often a deep and lasting one. It is true that appearance does not make the man, but it is also true that others cannot look through us to see how good we really are. They must get their first impression by what they see.

Habits of good appearance, which include clothing and grooming, are, therefore, very important in the desirable personality pattern.

The second system of habits is that of talk. It pertains to the voice. Again it can be said that voice does not make the man. But we cannot get away from the fact that it makes a tremendous impression on the reactions of others, good or bad.

The third is the very extensive system of habits that embraces all our other actions, thoughts, attitudes, and moods. These are the traits that we use as a valid basis for the analysis of a man's personality and character. Whereas appearance and voice are external habits, this third system of habits is the heart of the real personality of an individual. These make the man what he really is.

It is important that the good habits within all three systems be cultivated if we wish our relations to others to be good. Appearance and voice are reacted to first, and leave a deep impression. But it is our other actions, thoughts, moods, and attitudes such as friendliness, cheerfulness, sincerity, dependability, unselfishness, optimism, helpfulness, enthusiasm, and honesty, that assure permanently good reactions.

AS YOU WOULD A FRIEND

There are few things that contribute more to the pleasantness and effectiveness of our daily lives than does the habit of treating every individual with whom we associate as if he were a friend of ours.

The near magical results of this habit in both our personal and business lives is easily explainable. If we analyze exactly what we do when we are in communication with a personal friend, we will see why this kind of behavior will bring us success regardless with whom we deal or what we wish to accomplish.

When we are dealing with a personal friend we avoid artificial "fronts." We accept him as he is, and take it for granted that he accepts us as we are. We place all our "cards on the table," as the saying goes, and keep none in hiding, or in reservation up our sleeves for use in case of an unexpected move or deal.

We are cordial in our dealings with him. We greet him with a smile on our face and in our eyes, and keep him assured of our friendliness by repeated smiles as we talk or listen to him. He is our friend, and as such we understand and accept each other, and feel confident and secure in our mutual relationships.

What is equally characteristic of our behavior to a friend is that we are helpful to him. This is perhaps the highest test of our relationship. It requires thoughtfulness, and often some kind of extra effort or even sacrifice on our part. It means that we give him something of ourselves or of our service to help him fulfill his needs. In fact, we have a tendency to anticipate the needs of a friend, and then of doing something about these needs without being asked or requested by him.

If we were to practice in our business dealings only these few traits of the many distinctive of our relationships with our friends, we probably would be surprised at the success of our operations. To be natural, to be cordial, to be thoughtful or helpful, and to be so constantly in all of our relationships, is the simple magic that leads inevitably to business as well as to personal success.

All that our associates or customers want of us is that they can feel at ease in dealing with us; that they will be treated with cordiality and understanding; and that they can feel secure in the knowledge that they will be counseled and helped toward the best possible fulfillment of their needs.

This we can accomplish simply by treating each associate and customer with the same friendliness, consideration, and thoughtfulness that permeates our relationship with a personal friend.

WHAT IS SUCCESS?

Success is probably one of the most common of the goals of men, yet seldom does man attempt clearly to define for himself exactly what it is.

We all want it, yet few of us know exactly what we want. We expend on it a lifelong effort, yet do not know precisely what we are looking for, nor what path to take to reach it.

In America we vaguely associate it with job progress, or with the accumulation of riches. Parents point with pride to their son who has a good job. They speak of him as being successful. A daughter marries well if she marries a man of means. Men of moderate incomes regard with respect and honor the individual who has amassed great wealth. To them he is eminently successful.

Yet that, by itself, is not an absolute criterion of success in life. Would not emotional balance, moral integrity, cultural advancement, and a host of other personal and social qualifications have to be considered as a part of the measure of success?

Can a person be considered successful no matter what his accomplishments are, if he is spiritually barren, emotionally unstable, or intellectually sterile? Is he successful if he is socially misplaced, or if his family is unhappy? Is he successful if he lives only for himself and his own selfish gain and advancement?

Is the sole yardstick of success such a thing as power, prestige, influence, standing in the community, education, or for that matter, a combination of all of these? No, it is not, for even with these there could be misery, unhappiness, moral corruption, and ineffectiveness.

As far as I know there is only one way of defining and measuring success. It is doing one's best to make the most of oneself. It is not something that can be measured in relationship to the accomplishments of others. It is an individual matter and must always be determined by the degree in which a specific person has reached his own highest potentialities. In line with this, a person of great accomplishment may still be a failure if he is functioning below the best of which he is capable. And one of small accomplishment is an outstanding success if he is performing at the level of his maximum potential stature.

It is doing and being one's best that is success, and it is pure folly to measure it in relation to the accomplishment of others, or to determine it by any other standards. We are all different in potentialities, and each must determine the degree of his success by how completely he has realized his own particular individuality.

APPRECIATION THE BASIS FOR HAPPINESS

There are two essentials for happiness. The first is that we have the things that can give us peace of mind and contentment. The second is that we know or are consciously aware of the fact that we have these things.

Of the two, the second essential is by far the more important. It is the absence of a conscious awareness of the blessings with which we are bestowed or surrounded that is the chief factor in human unhappiness. It is the primary thing that keeps millions of us from appreciating the many satisfying and fulfilling possessions and experiences of our daily lives.

If we were to develop the habit of awareness of the favorable and munificent factors that are the very substance of our lives, most of us would be supremely happy. If we were to peg these in our minds and form a proper appreciation for them, we could not be otherwise than happy.

Happiness in the final analysis is no more than a state or condition of appreciation. It is recognizing our blessings and rejoicing in them. It is being thankful for that which we have but which need not be given to us, such as: our lives, our families, our food, our opportunities to work, our freedom to think and worship as we like, or, in other words, our opportunities to develop ourselves physically, mentally, culturally, and spiritually.

Being happy means not taking for granted the so-called commonplace things and occurrences. It means recognizing the fact that these are not ours by inherited right, and that they can be taken away. It means swelling with appreciation for the essential things we have, and to not moan about the accidental things we don't have. It means looking at life in terms of invaluables, and not in terms of incidentals.

We can look at the house which is our home, for instance, with deepest thankfulness and appreciation for the love, and comradeship, and security in which it enfolds us; or ignoring these, we can look at it in terms of the Cadillac which does not stand on its driveway. The one is happiness; the other is the absence of it.

And so it must forever be. Happiness is largely a matter of appreciation for the things that we have. But, since appreciation rests on awareness, it is essential that we recognize and acknowledge to ourselves specifically each and all of our many blessings.

The heavens could open and shower upon us all its richest gifts and favors, but if it withheld from us the sense of awareness and the sense of appreciation, its munificence would be barren and wasted. And this is precisely in part what the heavens has done. It has showered upon each and every one of us priceless gifts—priceless because they are the essential ones to our happiness. But we, the human beings, take them for granted as commonplace things. We close our mental eyes to their presence, and, consequently, fret and whine our lives away because of the incidental things that we think we want but do not have.

GETTING OTHERS TO GO ALONG WITH US

Most of us who are today in management or selling realize that to motivate people to go along with us in whatever objectives we have in mind, we must somehow or other satisfy for them one or more of their basic needs.

We understand that these basic needs of man fall largely within two classes. They are his survival needs and his ego-satisfaction needs.

The first are material ones, such as the need for food, shelter, clothing, and all other such things that help man to sustain his physical life.

The second are psychological needs such as the desire to belong, to be recognized, to be important, to be loved, and to love.

Experiences in leadership, whether it be in a business organization or in one's own family, and experiences in salesmanship, teach one quickly that there is no satisfaction of a need that will drive man more irresistibly into action than is that of his need to be important. With his whole heart and soul man yearns to be somebody, and he will most surely do the bidding of any person who will sincerely give to him the feeling that he is important.

Since this is an accepted and proved experience, would it not be just a matter of plain common sense that all of us make a more continuous effort to help the other person feel the sense of importance that he so deeply craves and wants?

And since no man can become successful by himself, or without the good will and cooperation of other people, is it not simple wisdom to try to get this cooperation in the most effective way known?

There are many ways in which we can make others feel more important. To say a word to them by way of recognition when they have done something in a superior way, or have tried hard to do a particularly good job, is one way to accomplish this aim.

Another way is to find out what people are interested in and then to get them to talk about these interests. To inquire of others about their jobs, their hobbies, and families; to ask them for their opinion and suggestions; and to ask them to do something for us, are never-failing ways of showing people that we think they are important.

To talk about them and not about ourselves; to look for superior traits or qualities in them, and then to say something to them about these qualities; to express appreciation for the things they do for us—even for the little routine and expected things, inevitably warms their hearts with a feeling of "counting," of being somebody important.

In general, the way of making people feel important is a matter of sincerely thinking, talking, and acting in terms of the interests, and likes, and accomplishments of the other person. For our own success and happiness it should be our aim in our relationship with others to get them to think more highly of themselves.

MAN'S MOST URGENT DRIVE

Man within himself is motivated in many ways to try to bring out the best that is in him.

He is urged on by many drives both tangible and intangible. His wants and desires are many, and anything that promises him the satisfaction of any of these is a stimulant that induces him into greater activity.

For instance, among the first of his basic wants is the desire to obtain food, clothing, and shelter for himself. Any activity, consequently, that holds out to him the promise of the means of physical support is a motivation to him. By his nature he is moved to do that which gives him what he wants.

Just as he wishes to support himself, so also in a more or less degree of intensity does he desire the opportunity to grow and develop, a pat on the back for a job well done, the respect of his fellow men, and the feeling of "counting," and of belonging.

All these things and many others are important to him. Without them there is no real meaning or satisfaction in his life.

Of all his desires, however, there is none that can exceed in importance his desire to be able to give to his wife and children a higher and more elevated plane of living.

It is for those whom he loves that he wishes most. It is for them that he strives to reach his highest level of performance. Recognition for his work and increased remuneration for greater accomplishment are significant to him mostly because they are the means by which he can give to his family a higher standard of living, greater educational and cultural opportunities, and the social prestige that gains acceptance for them in their community.

It is a man's family unit—his home, his wife, and his children—that is the most important thing in life to him. No security, no pats on the back, no forms of personal fame mean much to him except in terms of what they will do to further the well-being and happiness of this trio around whom his heart revolves.

It is in his devotion to them that he satisfies the most urgent of his basic needs—to love and to give himself in service for someone's greater happiness.

THE PRINCIPLE OF GIVE AND TAKE

Living and working together is a very satisfying experience if there is a proper balance of give and take among the members of the partnership or group.

Wherever we have happy, contented, and productive partnerships of human beings, we find that they have a common denominator. It is a willingness and a desire on the part of the members to complement one another; to share with the others; and to give full value in return for what is received. It is a sense of mutuality of benefits to be received, and a corresponding one of mutuality of contributions to be made.

Unsatisfying relationships among people, on the other hand, are usually characterized by someone's wanting and taking more than his share, or by giving less than he receives. They are the result of an infantile participation on someone's part in a situation that calls for adult relationships.

It is this kind of one-sided participation that is frequently responsible for the failure, or at least for the less than full fruition of many kinds of cooperative relationships be they marital, family, social, or business. Some member or members lack a sense of give and take. They have not developed a concept of maturity in attitude or action. In plain words, they have not fully grown up.

To ask other persons or another person to assume our responsibilities; to grasp for ourselves the recognition and rewards that are by right those of the other person; to use the power of body, wealth, or position for self-aggrandizement;

to get our way or to accomplish our ends regardless of the inconveniences or disadvantages that accrue to the other person; to expect the other fellow to give more largely than we ourselves hope to give; all these are ways of upsetting the give and take balance of life.

It is probable, too, that most conflicts in human interrelationships stem in some measure from someone's wanting to take or receive more than he is giving. They stem from someone's grasping for the benefits without paying proportionally for them in effort, service, devotion, or love.

It is safe to say that most of our daily frictions, jealousies, resentments, and frustration would be eliminated if we all accepted fully the principle of give and take, and acted accordingly towards one another. To take only in proportion to what we give, and willingly to accord to the other fellow the right to receive what he has earned through his efforts and accomplishments, is the basis for adult human relationships.

On the other hand, to want more than we have coming to us or to take from the other fellow what he deserves, is the way of an infant and creates an unsatisfying and thwarting relationship with our fellows.

LET'S FACE IT

It is unfortunate that so many of us will not face the fact that we are never going to be fully successful and happy until we have learned the great lesson of giving ourselves to others. The single most important principle in life is that if we wish to find ourselves we must first lose ourselves in service and devotion to someone or something outside of ourselves.

This is not a theory. It is a law of life as inexorable in the spiritual realm, as is the law of gravitation in the physical world. No life can be anything but narrow and empty unless it is expended by thoughts, words, and deeds that are not centered on itself but rather on things outside of itself.

Mankind is the business of every man. Every individual human being is his business and responsibility. Better human relations is his business. Every single one of us, for instance, must make it his business and accept it as a personal responsibility to teach the precepts, and through the example of our own personal relations set the pattern among men, of human interrelationships that are based on understanding, on tolerance, on justice, on equity, on the respect for the natural rights of man, and on the deep realization of the God-bestowed dignity of every single human individual.

There is more involved in our good human relations than our own personal success and happiness, and well-being. Ultimately, the thing at stake is the evolvement of civilization and humanity so that in time all mankind will live in the full brotherhood of man.

But we must give in one way or another if we seek fulfillment of our own lives. The very least that an individual can do is to give back to life in the same proportion to that which he has received from it. It is not permitted to all of us to give greatly of ourselves. This is a privilege that God grants to only a few. No man, however, can expect to find satisfaction and happiness unless he gives to others in the same measure that he gives to himself.

Dr. William Menninger expressed it beautifully in a recent television appearance when he said: "I just wish more people recognized for their own mental health that they're going to have to lose their soul if they're going to save it."

THE PRODUCT AND THE BY-PRODUCT

It is our deep and sincere belief that many of us do not obtain more of the material riches of life, simply because we work too directly and specifically for them.

We take a job in an office to earn so much money a week. Or we manufacture a product because we can sell it at a certain profit. Or we sell an insurance policy since it brings us a stipulated commission.

Obviously, we perform these activities because we have to make a living, or because we want some additional luxuries and comforts for ourselves and our families. And there is no argument about the correctness of our purpose in doing this. It is both our duty and right.

The thing, however, that is not generally remembered is that the money earned is really only a by-product of our labor. The purpose of the activity, or the real product is the fulfillment of a need that somebody has for the work we do, the article we manufacture, or the commodity or intangible that we sell.

Somewhere, somebody has a need for what we have to offer. Somewhere this offering helps people to exist or to live better. And for the giving of it we are compensated in a tangible way with money. But the product is the satisfaction of somebody's need; the by-product is the material compensation we get. Without the product, there is no by-product.

What we need to do to obtain greater riches is to fulfill more needs in a more satisfying way, or to give greater service. "I have a job to be done," that is where more emphasis must be placed; not on "How much will it net me?" The law of compensation takes care of the returns. It pays in proportion to what we have given effectively to cover the needs and wants of humanity.

The greater and more frequent our contributions, the greater and more frequent are the returns; the more satisfying the service, the more satisfying is the compensation; the more we give, the more in proportion do we get back. That is the law, and he who understands it, knows that great riches are the result of great and effective giving.

The by-product is extremely important, we admit. But as anyone acquainted with production processes knows, a by-product is possible only because of the manufacture of a main or first product. And so it is with riches. They are a By-Product of Service.

To be deeply interested in one's work is the best possible assurance of success in it.

As a rule, we become interested because we see in a particular work or job the way to the achievement of something that is of great importance to us. It could be that through it we see the way to the raising of the standard of living of our families. Or it could be a way to obtain desired status, fame, recognition, position, or material wealth. Or again it could be that in it we find a spot of usefulness among men, a way of being needed, or a way of giving ourselves in service.

From interest springs enthusiasm, and where there is enthusiasm there is devoted and sustained effort. If there is a way to success, enthusiasm finds it, and is cowed by few difficulties or obstacles. It enlists the whole body and soul of man to gain its coveted objectives. Enthusiasm—earnestly to will to achieve what is important to him—is the divine fire that inspires man to rise above brute existence.

Unfortunately, enthusiasm can be destroyed through continuous unrewarded effort. Since it feeds on evidence of progression, it dies when hope of progress is withheld from it. If, after long effort, an individual sees no progress forward, he loses the will to achieve. With it, too often, he dies as the real person he is.

Enthusiasm, to be sustained, must be fed with the food that satisfies the hunger that gave birth to it. If we would keep it alive and thus motivate men to their highest performance we must, as a consequence, do two things. We must find the source of their interest and enthusiasm. In other words, we must find out what they wish and expect to achieve. And secondly, by helping them move closer to their objectives we must keep fresh in their hearts the hope of ultimate and complete achievement.

To help our loved ones and our work associates keep their hearts afire with enthusiasm is one of the most remunerative contributions we can make to them. It is richly rewarding, both for them and for us whose lives are interwoven with theirs.

LOOK FOR THE REASON

When things are not going the way they should in our lives, there is a reason for it.

One of the most ancient of recognized philosophical axioms is that behind every effect there is a cause.

The axiom applies to the human equation. It is true in the life of each and every one of us. When things go right, for instance, it is because we have supplied the causes that make them go right. On the other hand, when things don't go the way they should there is a sequence that explains it.

In other words, there is a reason for our successes and failures. Somewhere in the background there is a fact, or a series of facts, that explains what is happening. Success or failure, happiness or misery, content or discontent are not fortuitous. They are brought about by specific factors, usually the doings of our own which we individually can control if we wish.

Personal or business success or failure is not accidental. It is caused. Yet we have the tendency to make ourselves believe that our failure, especially, is a happenstance. If we are not getting ahead on our jobs, if we are not making the sales we should, or if we are not earning the money we need to provide a proper living, we like to think of it as our poor luck or fortune. It just happens that way. Yet the fact is that it does not just happen that way. There is a reason for it.

It boils itself down to the fact that we have a problem, and if we wish to change the course of things, we must do something about that problem. This much is certain—closing our eyes to its existence will not solve it. The first step in its solution is obviously to recognize that it does exist. That is half the battle.

Then the second step is to look for the cause of that problem. It is to check into our character, personality, working habits, and into our daily habits of living to find the weakness, the deficiency, or the omission that is responsible.

Obviously, the third step is to do something about it. It is to root out, or to eliminate, or to correct that which causes our lives to be ineffectual, or our efforts to go amiss.

Hiding our heads in the sand to avoid admitting or facing a problem does not correct it. Blaming the problem on fate or on circumstances is not a cure. It is merely an aspirin or perhaps a sedative. Doing nothing to correct the cause of the problem is being fatuous. Problems do not correct or solve themselves. They are eliminated only by the active and positive correcting of what causes them.

If we wish to change an existing situation in our lives, we must change the conditions or causes that are responsible for it. If we wish to cure a physical headache, we must find and change that which causes it. So it is with life's headaches. We must find the causes and remove them although it may require surgery.

BREAD AND THE CIRCUS

The rulers of ancient Rome kept the populace from becoming unruly by providing them with bread and the circus or the games. Juvenal, the satirical poet of the time, speaks of bread and the circus as, "The only two things all men want."

Bread was provided as a necessity for existence. The games and gladiatorial combats, on the other hand, were held periodically to make that existence endurable. Their chief purpose was to divert the minds of the people off themselves and off the oppressions and hardships that were their lot.

What is significant about this practice to us, however, is that we have here several thousand years ago a recognition of a principle that we consider as quite a distinctively modern one. It is that man cannot live by bread or work alone. He must, if he wishes balance in his life, have also the games or some kind of relaxing play or fun. Work provides the bread to keep his body alive, but play is one of the vital ingredients that helps keep the body healthy, and assures as well the mental and emotional stability of the whole person.

Life, we must admit, is much more work than play, but to make it all work without the relaxing and balancing activity of play or fun is to court disaster. It is to make of oneself a breeding ground for excessive fatigue, boredom, physical ill health, and mental and emotional instability.

Man needs to play at times, preferably a short time each day. It brings about physical relaxation which gives his body an opportunity to build up new strength and vitality for the work that is ahead.

It, too, takes man's mind off himself, and his problems and worries. And that is perhaps the most important therapeutic value of play, for a man must forget about himself and his problems before his mind can clean house and revitalize itself.

Play, according to Aristotle, famous philosopher of the fourth century B.C., is anything that we love to do for its own sake. The important thing about it is that we must love to do it, so that we lose and forget ourselves in the activity. It must free us of ourselves. It must free us, for a time, of our tensions, conflicts, and anxieties, so our whole being has a chance to rest itself and to gain new strength.

The harder a man works, and the greater his problems are, the more important it is that he play often, if only for a short period at a time. It will enable him to come back to his job and his problems with more vitality and with a clearer vision. Emotionally, too, he will be refreshed. Play is a vital activity in his life and man should look upon it as essential and indispensable if he wishes to function regularly at his highest potential level.

A WAY TO PERSONAL SECURITY

In one psychological way, man's eviction from paradise was the single greatest thing that ever happened to him.

It shifted him from the position of being the dependent receiver of a bounteous paternalism, into the independent earner of all things bountiful through the activity of his own labor.

Perhaps man sinned because he was in rebellion against an unbearable psychological situation. He sat in the lap of luxury. All things were his for the taking. But, to continue to keep these things, he had openly to recognize the fact that they were his, not because he had a right of possession to them, but rather because someone had made them available to him under one condition. He must not eat a certain fruit. In other words, he had no real lasting independence, dignity, or security, for he had not earned what he was enjoying.

On the other hand, perhaps, the Creator of man planned it this way to teach him, in the very beginning of his existence, the most fundamental law of life. Perhaps it was here, at the very inception of man, that his God wanted to teach him how to walk upright with dignity and greatness.

The fundamental law of life is that man must earn what he receives if he wishes to live with dignity, and independence, and security. A corollary of it is that he who takes that which he does not earn through the sweat of his brow, or his brains, or his heart becomes a weakling, an insecure and crawling slave.

The great blessing that was bestowed on man in exchange

144

for his uneasy tenure of a physical paradise, was a deep desire to create and to accomplish, so that through his own efforts he could establish the right to what he needed and wanted.

Man still has available all of the abundance of paradise, but with the added privilege of earning it. He is not dependent upon the whim of others to enable him to possess and enjoy what he wants. All things are his for the earning. But he must work, and when he does so he not only gets the material things he wishes, but also realizes and fulfills himself as a complete and balanced human being.

No normal healthy human being wants anything for nothing. He wants no generosity showered upon him. He wants no paternalistic treatment from his employer. He wants only what he has earned, but he wants it in full measure. He is not dependent upon the munificence of others. He earns what he gets. His is the only real security, for its basis is within himself and his ability to work and accomplish.

Man, of course, can live off the labors of others. But when he does so his personality disintegrates and decays. He becomes a parasite, a whining and frustrated weakling. He must kowtow to others for what he needs. Let man, however, feel the challenge of creating his own life, and of getting what he needs through his own labors, and he becomes strong, virile, and confident. He has found the way to dignity, independence, and security. His life is his own.

INDUSTRY IS INDISPENSABLE

Although it is almost a cliché to say that the three qualities that make for success are knowledge, integrity, and industry, it is yet a fact that this trio constitutes the most effective formula for success known.

Knowledge is the fundamental factor. Integrity is the most important. Industry is the indispensable.

It is obvious that without knowledge or skill we cannot accomplish anything. First, we must know how to do something. It is on this basis, for instance, that every job is set up. There must be a production of some kind which is the result of knowledge and skill.

Permeating all our activity, however, there must be a second factor, which is integrity. Whatever we do must be in line with certain fundamental laws that safeguard the interests and the welfare of all men. We must, in other words, do what is right, and equitable, and just.

The indispensable factor in success, however, is industry. Without it neither knowledge or integrity is of much avail, since it is only through industry that we expose these to possible fruition.

Knowledge or skill, for instance, is useless unless it is applied. Of what value is the skill to operate a lathe, let us say, if the possessor of the skill does not apply it towards some useful production through the actual operation of a lathe? Of what value to an insurance agent is knowledge of insurance, and skill in selling, and integrity in dealing with others, if he is too indifferent or lazy to call on people, and thus expose his abilities and his integrity in the motivation of a prospect? Even a surgeon's training and skill is valuable only in the operating room.

It makes no difference how well an individual is equipped by nature or education to accomplish things, if he does not apply himself his powers will be wasted. Fruition of talents comes only to him who applies himself to his work with enthusiasm and devotion.

No one can last long in any responsible job if he does not have knowledge and integrity. But it is equally true that no one can make a success of such a job, even if he has knowledge and integrity, unless he likewise has industry. It is industry that is indispensable.

WHY MEN FAIL

It is a sad state of affairs that so many of us who fail do so because of factors that are within our own personal control to change or correct.

Even in our jobs, 76 per cent or more of us who fail do so because of deficiencies in personality which we could ourselves have corrected without too much effort.

A study made by one of our largest business management associations of 80,000 office and clerical employees in 76 highly successful corporations, shows that 76 per cent of us who fail to be promoted on our jobs, and that 89 per cent of us who are discharged, invite our own mediocrity or disaster by neglecting simple personality traits that we ourselves could change into desirable ones.

Survey after survey, scientifically made by many different individuals and institutions among a great variety of business organizations and life situations, prove to us incontestably that certain patterns of personality traits lead to success, and that others inevitably draw us into failure, regardless of the degree of technical skill that we have acquired. In fact, these same studies show that only about 15 per cent or less of those of us who fail do so because of lack of job knowledge or skill.

Thus, we fail because we permit ourselves to act habitually in some way or other in a manner that is not pleasing, or that sometimes may be offensive, to the other members of our group, whether it be a family group, or that of an office, factory, or field.

We fail because we do not take the time, or make the effort, to change one or more simple traits or habits that are unfavorably reacted to by our fellows.

We fail because we neglect to change an unacceptable way of acting into one that is acceptable to the people we live or work with. We openly invite failure because we do not change, for instance, such a habit as undependability into one of dependability; or a trait of unfriendliness into one of friendliness; or habits of laziness into diligence, untidyness into tidyness, noncooperation into cooperation, pessimism into optimism, dishonesty into honesty, gloominess into cheerfulness, or any one of other poor habits or traits into good ones.

It is sufficiently unfortunate that a few of us who fail must do so because nature did not give us the capacity to acquire the skill necessary for a certain kind of work. This is, however, nature's doing, and beyond our correction.

But the really sad thing is that most of us who fail, do so because we neglect to change personality traits that are harmful to us, but which are in our power to eliminate, or to modify into helpful and desirable ones.

THE OTHER FELLOW

To ourselves we are all very important persons.

And that is the way it should be. The individual who does not think highly of himself has little chance of making anything of himself. Nor does he have more than a paltry chance of winning the respect and esteem of his fellow men.

Our right to feel important is an incontestable one. We are important! As individual human beings we are unique entities. There is no one among our fellow men exactly like us. We are priceless. Our distinctive potential is unmatched. We fill a niche of our own in the universe that no one else can fill exactly as we do.

But, and this is a strange fact about life—the easiest way we can defeat ourselves with all of our importance is to let this self-importance go to our heads. It is to parade our self-importance before the world and demand homage. It is to claim it as a possession exclusive to us. It is to think, and talk, and act as if we were singled out from our fellow men in being important and in being superior to them.

To forget that the other fellow is as important in the eternal scheme of things as we are is a tragic mistake. To fail to recognize that he, too, is a unique entity, priceless in value, and unmatched in his distinctive potential, is our downfall.

To look upon ourselves as the central orb, and upon others as mere serving satellites, is the nemesis for many of us. It is like the wound on a tree through which oozes away the life-giving sap needed for the life of the whole tree.

And, too, literally speaking, the minimizing of the importance of others dries the well from which our own sense of importance quenches its thirst. It is known that what man thinks of his own importance is not enough to assure him that he is so. He must have it confirmed by the words and actions of his fellow men. Men, however, do not give us sincere and satisfying recognition on the basis of how important we think we are. They give it to us largely on how important we make them feel that they are. They, too, think of themselves as the center of the universe. Recognition to them also is the wellspring on which their egos feed.

Subordinating the importance of others in our desire to confirm our own, defeats the very thing that is most important to us—the feeling of assurance that we are important. Since this feeling can be satisfyingly confirmed to us only through the recognition that others express towards us, to assert our importance at the expense of that of others is a deadly human error.

Yes, the other fellow is important too! As an individual human being he is a unique entity. There is no one among all of other men exactly like him. He is priceless. His distinctive potential is unmatched. He fills a niche of his own that no one else can fill exactly as he does.

And what is vital to us is that to help him confirm to himself his essential importance is the only way we can get satisfying confirmation of ours. It is the other fellow who will feed or starve us according to what we feed unto him.

SEPARATING THE MEN FROM THE BOYS

A first step in establishing effective human relationships is that we separate the men from the boys.

We effectively relate ourselves to others not on the basis of what presumably they are as individuals, but rather on the basis of what they actually are. To be effective we cannot deal with a boy as if he were a man, nor with a man as if he were a boy, and expect desirable results.

It is thus essential that we know the stature of development of the individual with whom we deal. If we are dealing with a mature man, we relate ourselves to him as such. If we are with an adolescent, our relationships must be on the basis of adolescence. If we are with an infant, it must be in terms of the toys with which an infant plays.

To deal with a human being on a level above or below his actual stature of adultness is an abortive relationship. It can never be a satisfactory one. Frequently it is a very damaging one.

Dealing with others on the wrong level is largely brought about by the very natural human error of judging maturity by the chronological, physical or mental age of an individual. By, assuming, for instance, that an individual of a certain physical age has a corresponding age of maturity as a person, we deal with him on the level of that age.

Unfortunately, however, the maturity age of a human being as a person is largely an emotional matter. It has no necessary relationship with chronological, physical, or mental age. It has to do with the growth of an individual from childish self-

152

centeredness and dependency into socially responsible independence. It is a matter of his reactions to life, his attitudes, his set of values, and his sense of personal responsibility.

The end result is that each individual has a maturity complex distinctively his own in which there can be wide differences between his physical and his emotional maturity. He may be physically an adult, but emotionally a child, an adolescent, or a man. In human relationships with him we must, however, deal with him largely in terms of the emotional being he is.

Simply but very inadequately expressed, this means that if we want to get along with him and motivate him we must play with the toys he values and in the manner in which he likes to play with them. If he happens to be an emotional adolescent who wants his own way, resents direction, knows all the answers, and craves to have himself looked upon as a superior being, that is what we have to deal with. These are his toys and we must relate ourselves to him in terms of these toys.

To deal with him as we would with an individual who has grown into emotional adulthood would be to frustrate our purposes. It would probably invite antagonism and resentment to us. On the other hand, to deal with an emotional adult as if he were an adolescent would be equally futile and frustrating.

Obviously, then, the first step to effective human relationship is to separate the men from the boys and to deal with each according to his emotional stature.

THE BIG FOUR

We suppose all of us have wondered sometime or other, if there is not some particular way of living that would assure us a reasonably contented and happy personal life.

As a possible answer to this, I should like to offer for your consideration the activities often called "The Big Four." Frequently these are referred to as "The Things That Men Live By."

It has been believed from ancient times that within the compass of these activities lie all the satisfactions man needs to maintain the balance and equilibrium necessary for a complete and contented life.

These big four areas of activities are: Work, Worship, Love, and Play. It is in the exercise of these, each in its proper proportion, that we find the satisfactions of our basic needs. It is also through them that we obtain many of the extra things that all of us individually have learned to want and desire for a still richer life.

It is through the first of these, Work, that we acquire our material necessities and luxuries. It is also generally through it that we satisfy our basic need for craftsmanship, or our need to create—to produce something with our hands, our brains, or our personalities.

And, then, it is through Worship that we satisfy the race-old yearning of reaching upward to a Power greater than ourselves. It is only through it that man, realizing his inadequacies, can find security. It is man, the limited, drawing strength from the Unlimited.

And it is only through Love, the third activity, that man becomes a man. It is frequently said that man must be loved. This is no doubt true, but, on the other hand, it is infinitely more important that man becomes the lover. Until he has crawled out of himself, and has learned to give himself for the good and greater happiness of others, he has not matured, and has not begun the process of realizing his potential greatness.

And finally comes Play, which is perhaps the most under-rated and neglected of the great four. By Play we mean doing something just for the joy of doing it, be it throwing a ball, tending a flower bed, or painting a picture. Play is the great balancer. It is the relaxer, the destroyer of tensions. By taking our mind off ourselves and placing it on what we love to do, it saves us, as it were, from ourselves. It is the time one takes to permit one's soul to catch up with himself.

So as a recipe for daily living, we give you the Big Four: Work, Worship, Love, Play.

A MEANS OR AN END?

Some of us think of money in terms of life. Others think of life in terms of money.

There is a great difference between the two. In the first instance, money is a means. In the second, it is an end in itself.

In the one it is a means of exchange or barter. We give certain amounts of it in exchange for the products of someone else's labor or thought. In other words, we buy something with it to sustain life or to add to its livability. The more we have of it, the more of certain kinds of things we can add to our lives. If properly chosen, these can make life much richer and more worthwhile.

But if, on the other hand, we look at life in terms of money, that money can become the frustration and defeat of it. Life is bigger than money or any form of material wealth. Since it is mental, emotional, and spiritual, as well as physical, it requires many satisfactions that cannot be purchased.

Trying to satisfy its many needs through what money can buy leads to satiety and surfeit. Life to be fully nourished and sustained needs, too, that which comes from friendship, love, character, integrity, and service. It needs beauty, truth, justice, and faith.

All the money in the world cannot buy these things. No fortune can purchase the touch of a loving hand, or the smile of delight on a child's face. Nor can it purchase the peace and satisfaction that comes with the knowledge that one has given more to life than he has taken from it.

Perhaps one of the most serious consequences of looking at life exclusively in terms of money is that it ultimately fills man's heart with greed. He becomes obsessed with the desire for material acquisition. To him the dollar or its equivalent becomes the all-important thing. Craftsmanship, social contribution, and personal unfoldment and development become empty phrases.

Even friendship and love become circumscribed in terms of financial outlay or gain. Man's sense of values becomes distorted and base. He becomes incapacitated for any thought or action that transcends personal acquisition.

It is man's desire for money as a means to better living that is one of his greatest motivations. It is, however, his lust for money for its own sake and as a substitute for deeper inner values and aspirations that frustrates and defeats him.

Greed is one of the prime causes of mediocrity and failure.

THE SPECTER OF FAILURE

Failure, like success, is one of degree. It is a relative thing. No one fails completely.

The only satisfactory definition of failure is that it is functioning below one's capacity. The extent of failure is a matter of the degree in which we work and live below the best that we are capable of according to our individual natures.

It is not something that can be determined or judged by a standard of universal performance. It is an individual thing, and it is always a matter of an individual's actual performance measured against his highest potential. It is something that must be judged or determined in relationship to talents. It follows that the accomplishment which is a success for one, could possibly be considered a failure for another, or conversely.

We cannot logically determine that we are failures by the fact that our achievements are below those of our neighbor. This would be measuring a like performance against unlike individuals and sets of talents. If, however, our achievements generally fall below those of other persons in about our own social class or occupation, it should cause us serious concern. It is then imperative that we check ourselves to see if we are trying to do something that is too big for us, or if, on the other hand, we have a problem or a fault that is causing us to perform at a below par level.

Sometimes there are environmental factors that are responsible for our below-standard performance. It would be foolish to say that these factors are not frequently somewhat responsible ones in the degree to which we fail or succeed. Lack of personal capital, for instance, or poor financial conditions in our territories or throughout the country at large, family situations or exigencies, poor health, improper management relationships, lack of opportunities in our communities or in our jobs, social upheavals such as depressions and wars, or many other factors can be serious detriments to an individual's performance.

Generally speaking, however, these are seldom ruinous to men of strong personality and character. Man seldom needs to be the victim of his environment. He is equipped, at least potentially, to master his environment. A good many times his failure to do so is the result of faults in personality and character. Somewhere in his makeup there is the absence of certain desirable traits or habits, or, it may be, the presence of undesirable and destructive ones.

Since few of us human beings would consciously permit ourselves to harbor faults that invite failure, it seems to me that it must be the traits that we do not recognize as destructive, or the faults of whose existence we are not aware, that are most frequently the cause of our failures. Perhaps it would be well, then, to review occasionally the faults of personality and character that are known to bring failure to men, and to check ourselves for the possible presence of any of these faults in our habit patterns.

THE REFLECTION IN THE MIRROR

It is only natural that we sometimes wonder what the future will bring to us. Each of us would like to know what will happen to us in the days to come. For instance, will we be any more successful and happy a year from now than we are at present? Will we have a better job, more friends, more influence and prestige? Will we grow appreciably in stature and in maturity?

The answer to such questions can largely be predicted at any given period of time. There is no mystery about the future, whether it be tomorrow or a year hence. The future is what we see when we hold the mirror in front of us today. Unless we change what we see there, the picture of the future is clear before us. The inescapable fact is that we are tomorrow what we are becoming today.

It follows that if what we see in the mirror is not what we want it to be at some future date, we must change or alter what we are at this moment. The future is today. It is what we are now.

Fortunately, we can change the reflection in the mirror and, therefore, the future picture by changing the object whose reflection appears in the looking glass. Since we are that object, we must change ourselves, or accept what we see.

We change ourselves by the simple process of rebuilding the habits that make up our personality and character. Even the least change in these habits which are those of thinking, work-

160

ing, acting, and feeling, will change the reflection which is the picture of what is to be.

In simple words, this means if we want the future to be better than the past or the present, we must today take the dead spots and the kinks out of our personality and character pattern. There are no two ways about it. We change or the future remains unaltered.

A revision, for instance, in our working habits, or in our attitude toward life, or in our relationship with others, or in our sense of values will make us different persons. It follows that the reflection in the mirror will correspond, and that, therefore, again it will be a facsimile of the future.

It is true, of course, that a change in fortune or luck is sometimes a factor in the shaping of our future. But it is also an experienced truth that this change is more often than not the result of changes within ourselves and in our actions. It is we who largely create the "breaks" and the favorable concourse of events that we call fortune.

Change the reflection in the mirror and we change the future. Keep it as it is, and the future is pictured before us. We make our own choice.

FACING THE PROBLEM

When life is not going well for us, there is always a problem somewhere that explains it. This problem can be outside of us in our environment, or it can be within us in the form of personality or character faults.

But a problem there must be. Something is not right, for a human being can live successfully and happily if his activities are proper, and if he overcomes the things which block or interfere with the fruition of these activities.

Man's activities are his character and personality in action. The block to his activities are factors that arise from his environment. He can fail either because of the one, or the other, or of both.

His natural tendencies are to place the blame for his failures on the blocks that come from outside of himself. This tendency, however, is a very dangerous one, and it probably explains why so many men who act incompetently continue to do so throughout most of their lives.

The truth is that most of man's failures in performance are the result of activities that are the natural expression of his personality and character make-up. Generally speaking, it is we who bring about our failures through the activities that emanate from the inside of ourselves. Environmental blocks, of course, do exist, and they sometimes are responsible for failure. They may at times be insurmountable. This, however, is the exception and not the rule.

What any individual must do if he is failing, and if he wishes to change the course of his activities from failure to success, is to recognize first of all that he has a problem. This is basic. No human being can change his life for the better, if he does not awaken to the fact that he is not doing well and that there is an explanation for it.

Secondly, he must be exhaustive in gathering and examining the facts surrounding his life so he can determine the nature of the trouble. He must determine if it is within himself, or if it is in his environment, and specifically what the responsible factors are in the one or the other.

He must then find a way of changing these factors. It may be necessary to try out a number of solutions, to find one that will eliminate the problem. And finally when he has found the solution, he must apply it. In other words, he must make the corrections called for by the facts that he encountered.

But first and always, and most important, comes the recognition of the problem. It is half the battle. He who faces his situation squarely and admits to himself that there is something wrong, has gone a long way toward victory.

LACK OF SELF-CONFIDENCE AND FAILURE

—••❧❦❧••—

Lack of self-confidence keeps millions of individuals from accomplishing their maximum potential. In fact, it is so universally a deterrent to full human development that very few people ever reach beyond a small percentage of their potential possibilities.

Lack of self-confidence is, plainly speaking, an absence of faith in ourselves. Either we do not have a true picture of our greatness as human beings and as individuals, or we lack faith in our ability to be our great selves in competition with others, or with the various circumstances and factors of our environment.

It means that we are afraid to pit ourselves against the forces of life that make difficult the realization of our needs, and hopes, and dreams, and aspirations. More often than not it is a matter of not trying to obtain something because we are afraid that we will fail in the effort.

Overcoming lack of self-confidence is not too difficult if we will do the following three things: 1. Get a clear understanding of the innate greatness of ourselves by virtue of our being human beings and distinctive individuals. 2. Quit the habit of competing with others. 3. Act as if we were filled with self-confidence.

A little intensive thinking on our part, coupled with a careful analysis of our nature, should quickly impress us with the inherent greatness of our human nature. In fact, it should suffice for us to know that we are made according to the image of

164

God, and that we have that within us which demands that we walk upright and with confidence and courage.

In regard to the second point, we can think of no greater fallacy than our endless competition with others. We must realize that we are distinct individuals, different from all other people. We are unlike each other, and, therefore, can never do anything exactly as the other person does it. Man should compete only with himself and with the forces within him that keep him from the effort to be his best possible self. What counts is that we do our best. The other fellow's best has essentially nothing to do with our success or failure.

Finally, we overcome lack of self-confidence by acting as if we were confident. It is by outward action that the inner mood is formed, and he who acts confidently on the outside will eventually be so in the inside of himself. Act as if there were no doubt of your ability or of the success of your venture. Do this even if you are not able to rid your thoughts of misgivings and doubts.

Lack of self-confidence is, then, another of the factors that cause men to fail. It, like all such other factors, can be overcome and conquered. It is never necessary to fail because of causes that exist within ourselves. We have mastery over these if we want badly enough to succeed.

THE EMOTIONS THAT DESTROY

In a discussion about the importance of getting along with one's self, we mentioned certain emotions as being destructive of peace of mind and personal happiness. We stated that these destroyed our ability to get along with ourselves, and were, therefore, often at the root of our conflict with other people.

If one wishes to be at peace with one's self, it is of course necessary that he keep himself largely free from tensions, frustrations, feelings of insecurity, and from all other such mental and emotional disturbances that tend to incapacitate him in the free and full expression of himself.

There are a few emotions that are particularly disturbing to the human being, and that have been recognized from the dawn of civilization to be ruinous to him. They destroy not only his mental and emotional but also his physical health. They make it impossible for him to act and live objectively, or to have the wholesome reactions of a normal being to himself, to others, or to life in general.

The emotions we refer to are known as the deadly ones. They are fear, anger, hate, pride, and envy. Any one of these is cankerous, and if permitted to grow beyond bounds will destroy physical health, personality, and character.

The one that is most dangerous to us, not because of its greater malignancy, but rather because it is so universally present among men in an excessive degree, is fear. It, one may safely say, is the arch enemy of men. It ranks as the number one of the factors that keep man from realizing the complete fullness of his potential stature. It does more than any other one thing, or combination of things, to dwarf man in mediocrity or to cause him to fail completely in his life.

God created man the lord of all created things. He made him His supreme masterpiece. He gave him an upright body, a great intellect, a soul after His own likeness. He gave him all the faculties and powers to grow into a magnificent being equipped to shape for himself a high destiny.

Man, on the other hand, created fear, which makes of him a creeping thing, afraid to walk upright, afraid to accept the challenge of his own potential greatness. Man has made himself afraid by the goblins of his own thinking. He has permitted an instinct that was meant to help him survive, to possess and destroy him.

If man wishes to enjoy the full use of his great powers; if he wishes to be physically and mentally healthy; if he wishes to get along well with himself and with his fellow men; he must not permit fear, or hate, anger, pride, or envy to become dominant in his being. He must keep himself free of them, which he can do if he wishes.

THE WHY OF OUR INSECURITY

In this twentieth century we have made tremendous advances in technology.

Through these advances we have developed a science of mass production that has raised the standard of living even of our poorest families to excel that of the most fabulously rich monarchs of history.

No powerful Caesar, for instance, could have imagined such luxurious adjuncts to his living as the television, the electric light, the refrigerator, the automatic washer and dryer, the electric range, the radio, the air-conditioner, and all the other multiple appliances that we consider basic necessities in the modern home.

And to help our people feel secure in the possession of these, we have guaranteed annual wages, social security, labor laws, compensation laws, unions, group and commercial insurances, sick leaves, and a host of other devices. We build a fence around modern man so that he will not lose the income necessary to retain his high standards.

But for some reason we have not made man much happier or more secure than he was before. We have filled him with frustrations, tensions, and anxieties, and have utterly destroyed his sense of security. We have focused his thinking on material things, and have supplied these to satisfy his every desire for convenience and luxury. But in our urgency in mastering the technological sciences, we have neglected the science of humanity. We have made very little headway in our mastery of the science of man's relationship with himself or of his interrelationship with his fellows. We have failed in teaching people to live together in such a way that they are secure in their possessions from each other.

Thus in the midst of his material wealth, man cowers in fear and insecurity. Instinctively he knows that he is secure only if his conduct and that of his fellow men is right and just and unselfish. He knows that security lies not so much in things as it does in the ideals, values, attitudes, and beliefs that permeate and determine the conduct and interrelationship of man.

Man is insecure because he is not sure if he can trust his own behavior or that of his fellows. Nor can all the goods produced for him through our technological supremacy make him feel less insecure until human society has fully subscribed in practice to the principles of living expounded by the two great human engineers of the past, Moses and Christ.

The fact is that there is no real security for anyone unless all men live with each other in integrity, justice, compassion, and mutual consideration and love.

MAKING SALES

The expression "to make a sale" is a term wide and inclusive in its application. To apply it only to the act of successfully convincing someone to buy a product or commodity is to confine it to one of its incidental usages.

"Making sales" is what every successful and happy person does constantly. It is the process through which we get people to accept us, and to do what we consider needful or desirable for our welfare or advancement.

"Making sales" is to get others to want to cooperate with us in the accomplishment of our purposes and objectives. It is the basis for every successful human achievement. And nowhere it is of greater importance than in the activities of everyday life.

Essentially, "making a sale," or what is the same thing, motivating another to do what we wish him to do, involves three things. The first is that we must let the other person know what we want him to do for us. The second is that we show him how to do it. And the third, which is the most important, is that we must get him to want to do it for us.

All three of these are important. It is, however, the third which is the essence of the "sales" act. Unfortunately, it is, too, the third which most of us overlook or ignore. We take it for granted that other people want to do things for us. We forget that human beings by nature think and act largely in terms of themselves and their own interests, and are concerned primarily with what is of benefit to them.

To get others interested in cooperating in the fulfillment

of our needs and desires, we need to associate what we wish of them with something that is satisfying to their own wants. The fundamental, essential factor in all motivation is "What does the other fellow get out of it? Is there enough in it for him by way of satisfaction of personal needs and desires to make him want to do what we ask him to?"

In the field of supervision or leadership where group activities are involved, we call this morale. Morale is nothing more than the desire of each member of the group to do his very best for the accomplishment of the objectives of the group and its leader, simply because the material and psychological setting is such that each member gets out of his work what he wants in the way of basic personal satisfactions. He gives his best, probably unconsciously, because of what is in it for him by way of tangible and intangible satisfactions.

And so it is in every activity of life in which we need the cooperation of others. We get this cooperation by "selling" or motivating the other person on the basis of what is in it for him. It is not what we get out of it that counts in the "sale." It is rather what he gets out of it. *What is in it for him that will make him want to do our bidding* — that is the only sound "sales" approach.

SELLING ONESELF

Selling is the motivation of another human being to get him to do something we wish him to do.

The salesman accomplishes this motivation by presenting three things to his prospect: himself, the fulfillment of a need, and the product that fulfills the need.

The most important of these is himself, for if he sells himself, the other two follow more or less as a matter of course. If he succeeds in selling himself so that his prospect likes him, trusts him, and believes in him, his sale is over ninety per cent accomplished.

On the other hand, if he fails to sell himself, he will find it unlikely that the prospect will buy from him the fulfillment of a need, or the product that he offers as a way to fulfill that need.

So it is with life as a whole which is essentially for each of us a continuous sales activity. We are always selling ourselves in one fashion or another, whether we succeed or fail depends largely on our ability to motivate others to fulfill through us their essential needs.

We are constantly in the process of motivating others to do what we think is necessary or desirable for us to live a more complete life. We do this by selling ourselves, by showing others that they have a need for us, and by convincing them that we have the necessary knowledge and skills to satisfy that need.

It is of importance, of course, that we offer our qualifications and talents where there is a need for them. But their acceptance or use by others will in most instances be contingent upon whether they accept us and respond favorably to our personality and character.

Knowledge and skill is important to say the least, but there is no particularly high premium attached to them unless they are made marketable through the medium of a likeable and pleasing personality.

It is the selling of ourselves that counts. People will buy what we have to offer, if we have first motivated them to buy us as likeable, trustworthy, honest, and sincere persons. If they like us, and feel secure and safe in their association with us, they will go out of their way to let us fulfill their needs with whatever we have to offer them.

To sell oneself — that is the crux of all motivation and accomplishment.

SHARING OUR EGO

The following "Capsule Course in Human Relations" is significant as a way of living more successfully in that it gives us a concrete five-point method of winning for ourselves the good will and devotion of our fellow human beings.

1. Five most important words, which are words of appreciation: I AM PROUD OF YOU.
2. Four most important words, which are words of consultation: WHAT IS YOUR OPINION?
3. Three most important words, which are words of courtesy: IF YOU PLEASE.
4. Two most important words, which are words of gratitude: THANK YOU.
5. The most important word, which is one of cooperation: WE (Or the least important word: "I.")

The fact that all five points of this Capsule are ways of giving to others implied or expressed recognition of their importance, emphasizes again a basic tenet in human relations. It is one of the simplest yet most important ways of influencing and motivating the human being. *Man wants to be somebody, and he wants others to recognize that he is.* So strong is this desire within him, that he will give all the loyalty and devotion of his being to the individual or firm that gives him this recognition. He will give his best to those who help him attain mental stature.

In spite of the fact, however, that we realize the great compelling power of this simple giving of earned recognition, most of us still neglect or refuse to do so.

One can understand this neglect on the part of those who do not know of the ways of influencing others. Too often, however, one must look upon it as a symptom of some personal maladjustment. It makes us suspect the presence of extreme self-centeredness, actual inferiority, or an inferiority complex.

Self-centered individuals are too frequently wrapped up in themselves and their own satisfactions to have the time to think of the wants and needs of others. Actually inferior people, on the other hand, are afraid to give recognition, because by raising the stature of another, they feel that they diminish their own. And those with an inferiority complex are too concerned with efforts to compensate themselves for their imagined inferiority to have any thought for the other fellow. They frequently attempt to belittle him, in an effort to make themselves seem more important.

But the normal person should recognize in this giving of recognition a habit of utmost value, and one that generally costs the giver nothing. It requires no money, very little effort, and a minimum of time. *All it takes is a willingness to share a little of one's own ego.*

Rather than detracting from the personal prestige of the giver, it increases it. Rather than diminishing his stature, it causes it to grow. Rather than taking away his personal power and authority, it adds power and authority. For men will give their everything to the one who gives them stature through recognition.

This free giving of recognition, and the spontaneous doing of things to give stature, is important to the giver in another way. It brands him; it singles him out, for it is the unmistakable mark of the assured, confident, and matured leader. It is a trait that is never found in the weakling. It is distinctive of the strong and the great.

175

ACTING SUPERIOR BELITTLES OTHERS

It is often asked if there are some poor personality traits that are more detrimental to good human relations than others.

Although this query must be answered affirmatively, we believe that in doing so one should first re-emphasize that all poor personality traits have undesirable effects on our relations with others. Any one negative trait or habit can block the flow of our entire personality, and can result in unfavorable reactions to us.

We human beings have a tendency to notice in others what is defective rather than that which is normal. We tend, too, to ascribe to the whole of a personality what is only a defective trait within the whole. Thus we label an otherwise wholesome individual as sarcastic, undependable, or selfish, because in the pattern of his personality there is evidence of this particular undesirable trait.

Any poor trait can thus hurt us by dimming out our real personality, and by attracting attention to itself. Whether the reaction to us will be one of mere indifference or of definite dislike will depend on the trait with which we are identified.

Naturally, some traits or habits cause a more unpleasant reaction than others. Some create a feeling of distaste toward us, and cause people to shun association with us. Habits, for instance, that belittle others, or that make them feel afraid, insecure, or inadequate are the most detrimental to good relations.

One such habit is that of acting or talking superior to others. A name for it is egotism. Or in its most undesirable degree of development it is known as arrogance.

We believe that all of us will agree that arrogance is one of the most offensive of bad personality traits. It draws instant and deep resentment from those who are subjected to it, for it does to them what by nature they want most to avoid. It belittles them. It makes them feel inferior. It creates in them a sense of fear and insecurity. It takes people out of the center of the universe where they have placed themselves, and subordinates them into places of insignificance.

He who wishes to make the best of his relationship with others will avoid any semblance of the show of superiority. He will do and say the things that will build up the prestige of his fellows. He will learn the ways of making them think better of themselves; of making them feel more significant and important; of growing an inch taller in their own sights.

"The load of tomorrow added to that of yesterday, carried today, makes the strongest falter."

This thought is the basis of a philosophy used by many successful men to assure themselves that every bit of their energy and vitality is used constructively each day in the accomplishment of their purposes.

The philosophy of doing one's best each day, and of living strictly within the twenty-four hour cycle, was given prominence by the noted Dr. William Osler, internationally known philosopher and physician, and one of the most highly respected men of his era.

In a famous lecture to the students at Yale University in 1913, he added: "Touch a button and hear at every level of your life, the iron doors shutting out the Past—the dead yesterdays. Touch another and shut off with a metal curtain, the Future—the unborn tomorrows. Then you are safe—safe for today.

"The petty annoyances, the real and fancied slights, the trivial mistakes, the disappointments, the sins, the sorrows, even the joys—bury them deep in the oblivion of each night—and you will wake a free man with a new life."

And of the future, he said: "The future is today—there is no tomorrow. The day of a man's salvation is *now*—the life of the present, of today, lived earnestly, intently, without a forward looking thought, is the only insurance for the future."

Dr. Osler stated that the workers in Christ's vineyard were hired by the day; and that only for this day are we to ask for our daily bread, and that we are expressly bidden to take no thought for the tomorrow. He continued by saying that he is prepared to urge the literal acceptance of this advice, and that in the words of Carlyle, "Our main business is not to see what lies dimly at a distance, but to do what lies clearly at hand."

An Omaha surgeon who studied under this prominent medical teacher at The Johns Hopkins University made available to me his class notes in which he had recorded verbatim a statement of the ideals of Dr. Osler as they were given by the noted teacher in one of his class sessions.

As a way to more successful living, I give Dr. Osler's ideals in his own words:

I have had three personal ideals. One, to do the day's work well and not to bother about tomorrow. It has been urged that this is not a satisfactory ideal. It is; and there is not one which the student can carry with him into practice with greater effect. To it, more than anything else, I owe whatever success I have had—to this power of settling down to the day's work and trying to do it to the best of one's ability, and letting the future take care of itself.

The second ideal has been to act the Golden Rule, as far as in me lay, towards my professional brethren and towards the patients committed to my care.

And the third has been to cultivate such a measure of equanimity as would enable me to bear success with humility, the affection of my friends without pride, and to be ready when the day of sorrow and grief came to meet it with courage befitting a man.

179

LOOKING AT THINGS IN PERSPECTIVE

Too many of us waste our energy and vitality by excessive concern about things, which looked at in perspective, are inconsequential.

We let the mountains climb over our molehills because we look at each problem in isolation and not as an incident in relation to the whole of an enterprise or of life.

Even the smallest disappointment or frustration can look big to us if we look at it by itself and in terms of how it is affecting our lives at this particular moment. A change in the weather that defeats our plans for today; a sale that we fail to close; a promotion we did not get; current financial difficulty; sickness in our family; or any one of hundreds of things that are part of the ups and downs of a normal life can thus become an irritation of undue magnitude.

How often as we grow in years and experience do we look back with smiles at incidents that seemed tragic to us in our youths, or even in as short a period as a year or a few months before? As we viewed them then at the time of their occurrence, we looked at them in terms of the then present. Now, as we see them in relation to the whole, they seem small and incidental—simple hurdles that were part of the everyday course of life.

To look at everything in relation to its effect on the whole is one of the secrets of serene and confident living. He who does so soon discovers that very few problems, difficulties, or frustrations are of serious import.

He will see that rarely does the vexatious problem or situation of the moment have any bearing on the total picture of his life. Only once or twice in a lifetime does a man come face to face with a situation that is catastrophic in its possibilities.

All of us have problems and difficulties. Each day has within it some incident or situation that at the moment seemingly threatens our well-being and happiness. The wise man of experience, however, will view these in their relationship to the whole of his life. Their consequences and import to him will then appear in their true perspective. This in turn will keep him free from the irritation, vexation, and fear that beset most of us when vicissitudes disturb the even flow of our lives.

The wise man is thus able to face his problems objectively and with his full energies. He is able to seek a solution to them through intellectual processes, and not through subjective emotional stewing. He is thus able also to attack his problems with his full powers, since he has not made it possible for fear, irritation, and vexation to drain these powers of their rich vitality.

If, however, by chance he finds no solution to a particular obstacle or situation, he is still undisturbed, for he knows that when considered in relationship to the whole of life it is probably inconsequential.

A MISSION BEYOND HIMSELF

The most ancient of biological facts is that survival comes first. Any living organism desires first and above all the maintenance of its life. It is the deepest and most urgent drive of its nature.

Of man, it made the cave man a hunter; the nomad, a shepherd of flocks; the settler, a tiller of the soil; of man today, a farmer, a mechanic, a clerical worker, a professional man, or a business executive. It is the unrelenting urge that drives man on to production through his hands, his mind, and his ingenuity.

That existence comes first is, too, the first of motivating principles. Man is not seriously moved by any other need of his nature until he has secured for himself the means to exist.

It would, however, be a grave error to suppose that existence or survival is all for which a man works. It is merely the primal thing, but it is not by itself sufficient to give him a satisfying life, nor to make a dedicated worker out of him.

It is a necessity of his nature, but as Woodrow Wilson has so aptly stated it, "Necessity is no mother to enthusiasm. Necessity carries a whip. Its method is compulsion, not love. It has no thought to make itself attractive; it is content to drive. Enthusiasm comes with revelation of true and satisfying objects of devotion; and it is enthusiasm that set the powers free."

Looking at it, then, from the viewpoint of his work, a man who labors merely for an existence, is no more than a slave to his compelling physical needs. He will never be a worker of

182

great accomplishment. Mere existence does not arouse enthusiasm, and without enthusiasm there is no devotion or dedication, which is the wellspring of all great effort.

To become enthusiastic about a work requires other satisfactions than survival. In addition to it the worker must receive ego-compensations, and ultimately to make of him a dedicated worker he must receive a sense of service to his fellow men.

It is this sense of service that gives meaning and purpose to his efforts, and any work that does not give it eventually becomes a mere drudgery to man.

In other words, man will be fundamentally motivated to put in effort by the existence he gets out of it. He will be further motivated by the ego-recognition he gets in addition to the necessary income. But, ultimately to give his fullest efforts, he must find in that work a purpose and meaning that reaches beyond his personal gains. He must find in that job a means of extending himself into usefulness for his fellow men.

A job without meaning and purpose is a dead-end street. It may bring a mediocre existence, but it will never challenge man to great accomplishment. That requires dedication to a mission of usefulness beyond himself.

THE CHALLENGE TO SERVE

Twenty-seven centuries ago the prophet Micah answered the question that to earnest-minded men is the primal and basic one in the conduct of their lives.

The question is, "What must man do to make himself acceptable to his God from Whom he springs, and to Whom he must eventually account for the custodianship of his life?"

Succinctly, concretely, and clearly Micah gave the answer: "What doth the Lord require of you, but to do justly, to love mercy, and to walk humbly with thy God."

The pronouncement is definite. It leaves no room for quibbling. It permits no variances. It allows no deviations. It makes no provisions for extenuating circumstances. It makes no exceptions. To young and old, rich and poor, literate and illiterate, socially prominent and socially unknown, powerful and weak— to each and all, there is only one acceptable way of life: to do justly, to love mercy, and to walk humbly with God. For man to do otherwise is to gainsay his divine birthright. It is to forfeit the possibility of maturing into his potential stature.

But, in addition to the requirements of his God, the earnest-minded individual is, too, concerned with the expansion of himself in the fullest possible use of his potentials in the world of men of which he is a part. In other words, Micah has sharply defined for him the requirements of his God; but, the question that poses itself to man is what he must do beyond those requirements to reach full maturity in the use of his powers and talents for the ultimately greatest good of himself and of his fellow men.

Man's heritage, it is true, is from God, but it is among men on earth that he lives, and it is in his daily relationships with them that he must seek the full growth of his powers and of himself.

But what then, man asks, does living among men require of him in addition to that he act justly, loves mercy, and walks humbly with his God?

The answer comes not from the prophet of old, but rather from the silent voices of the millions upon millions of men and women of past ages who, through their hardships and sufferings, and who, through their ingenuity and courage, have set the stage of life for him. It comes, too, from the depth of his own mature heart: What does life among men require of you, but that you put back into this stream of life something to enrich it in return for that which you receive from it.

The answer, as was that of Micah, is succinct, concrete, and clear. It is simply that to live maturely he must give to life as well as take from life. He must give to it something to enrich it and enlarge it in return for the benefits he receives. It requires that he play the part of a man among the race of men. It requires that he forsake the role of an infant, and accept that of the mature adult. It requires that he give to life as nearly as possible in some kind of proportion to that which he receives from it.

The whole question of what is required of him to live maturely and fully can be answered with one word: *Serve.* It is to reach out from himself into the lives of men. It is to give as well as take. It is to give of himself through service in the affairs of men.

185

THE RIGHT OF CHOICE

A human being does not have to do anything that he does not want to. Of all created things or beings, animate or inanimate, he is the only one who has the right of choice.

This does not mean, however, that he can do or not do with impunity whatever he wishes, for every choice or act of his has consequences over which he has no control.

As an example, he does not have to eat unless he wants to. Nature, through the pangs of hunger, cooperates with him by creating the desire to eat. If he chooses, however, to go contrary to nature's urgings, he is able to do so. His is the choice—to eat or not to eat. The consequences of his choice, however, are not of his doing. If he eats, he lives. If he does not, he dies. Nature prescribes the results and they are arbitrary.

So it is, too, with his other choices. He does not have to live according to the Ten Commandments. No one can force him to, but if he does not so live it will be to the detriment of his personal and social well-being. The consequences, with certainty, will be unhappiness and failure. If that is the price he is willing to pay, the choice is his.

Nor can any man be forced to devote himself to bringing happiness to his wife and children. It is his privilege and his obligation, but if he chooses to neglect to do so, the choice is again his. But he cannot make this choice and at the same time have the affection and love of his family, nor the deep satisfaction that comes from bringing happiness to those for whom he is responsible.

So it is also with the management of a business or industrial organization. Because of the prerogatives of authority, management does not have to give to employees the satisfactions wanted by them from their jobs. It does not have to delegate responsibility and authority to them; it does not have to consult with them; it does not have to give them a sense of participation; it does not have to provide the opportunities for them to use their maximum skills and abilities. It does not even have to respect their rights and dignity. *But it does have to, if it wants individual and group efficiency, loyalty, and devotion from them.*

So in practically all of the aspects of life man has the right of choice in his actions. He has free will. He does not, however, have the right to a choice of consequences. These are ordained by whatever laws of nature or of life apply, and are inevitable and unalterable.

The harvest that men thus reap in their lives, they sow by the exercise of their choice of action.

SEEING THE GOOD IN OTHERS

—◆⟨|⟩◆—

Recognition of others, to be effective as a way of influencing people, must be sincere. It must be based on attributes that actually exist.

Insincere praising to help one gain certain selfish ends is flattery. It is not founded on existent qualifications. It is false recognition, and is generally detrimental to permanently good relationships.

There is no necessity, however, for resorting to flattery in dealing with people. We can always find nice things, good attributes, praiseworthy qualifications in other human beings if we earnestly look for them.

He who would develop the maximum skill in getting along with others, must then learn to look for the good things in them. He must train himself to see what makes an individual superior to other members of his group.

We doubt if there is a human being who is not superior in some way to his fellows. Every one of us has his particular good points: a physical attribute, a skill in doing something, a choice material possession, a beautiful flower garden; an attitude toward home, or work, or life; a particular social accomplishment, a highly desirable trait of personality, or any one or more of thousands of possible points of superiority.

And certainly there is no human being who is so hapless that he has nothing good or attractive about him. Men are never all-good or all-bad. There is always some of each in us, and we believe that experience would show that in the worst of us there is much more good than bad.

What we see in others is primarily a matter of what we are looking for. If we wish to see that which is unattractive, that is what we will find. But why look for the unpleasant, when we can enrich our human relationships, and add materially to our success and happiness, by directing our sights to that which is attractive, wholesome, or superior about the other person?

The superior or the good is there. But the trick is to look for it and to make it the basis of our appreciation of others. Once having developed this ability, it should be comparatively easy to form the habit of expressing recognition of it.

Look for the good or the superior. Sincerely say something about it when the opportunity comes. Do this without fail! And you will never be without multitudes who will follow wherever you choose to lead. It is a priceless ingredient in human relations!

SMILE! IT PAYS OFF

Most of us human beings are friendly people. We feel kindly toward our associates. We wish them well. We rejoice in their happiness and success; grieve with them in their misfortune.

It is only once in a great while that we find someone so little and so wrapped up in himself that he is indifferent to or hostile to his fellow beings.

Yet friendliness of feeling is in itself not a sufficient factor in our relations to others. To be really a positive and effective thing, it must be friendliness shown externally. It must be an external expression of an inward feeling.

It is obvious, of course, that others cannot see through us to see how we feel toward them. They have no way of knowing how we feel unless somehow we show it on the outside.

It is for this reason that it is so very important to develop the art of showing our friendliness. And friendliness is shown by being helpful to others; by being sympathetic, tolerant, and understanding.

But most of all, it is expressed through the simple act of smiling. Wise, indeed, is the individual who has developed this art or habit. For the smile is the natural sign of friendliness. It is the badge we wear on the outside to express our internal attitude. It is the symbol of warmth.

The smile, more than any other factor, breaks the "ice barrier" between us and our fellow human being. It dispels tenseness in human relationships. It creates "at easeness." It makes others feel "at home" with us. And people tend strongly to seek out and associate themselves with those with whom they feel "at home."

The smile is the symptom of internal health. It quiets fear. It creates trust. It gives assurance and security.

A smile is the key that opens the human heart.

It is safe to say that no other one thing will add more immediately to the richness of our daily lives than the cultivation of the habit of smiling.

Smile! Smile tall! Meet people with a smile! It pays off!

SAY THE NICE THINGS YOU THINK

Every human being is to himself the center of the universe. To him, everyone and everything else revolves around him. He is the all-important nucleus.

There are no natural exceptions to this. You—I—everyone whom we know, instinctively feels the same way. "The deepest principle of human nature" said William James, the great American psychologist, "is the desire to be important."

He who wishes to get along well with people will make full use of this deeply rooted desire to be the center of things—to be important—to be appreciated.

If he is wise, he will take himself out of that center as much as he can, and will permit the other fellow to occupy it to the fullest. He will take every opportunity to make his friend, his neighbor, or his business associate feel more important. He will give him sincere recognition whenever he can.

He will say and do the things that will make the other person think better of himself. He will make use of every opportunity to give others the feeling of "counting." For "to count," that is what all of us want most deeply. To stand out and to be recognized as being in some way above the mass of humanity is dearer to the heart of man than any other single thing. Man will do almost anything to gain the expressed approbation of his fellow men.

The way of wisdom, then, if we wish to get along best with our fellow man—if we wish to influence, motivate, and control

192

him and his actions, is to give him sincere recognition. It is to think, say, and do the things that will make him feel more important.

One reason we so often fail to do this is that we think too much in terms of ourselves and too little in terms of others, be they our family members, friends, employees, clients, or just plain fellow human beings. We have too much ego-concentration and too little "you" consciousness. We are so involved in our own comforts, social standing, material enrichment, position, play for power and status that we forget the sense of importance of the other fellow.

In other words, we are so wrapped up in our own little selves and our own little affairs that we do not take the time to say to the other person the nice things we think about him. And as a result, quoting from "The Fool's Prayer" by Edward R. Sill,
    The word we had not sense to say—
    Who knows how grandly it had rung!

It is not enough just to THINK nice things about others! It is necessary actually to EXPRESS to them through word and deed the nice things we think.

A PROFITABLE INVESTMENT

Let us, for the moment, look at good human relationships strictly from the selfish viewpoint.

Let us ignore completely what it means to the other fellow; how deeply satisfying it is to him; how it feeds many of his deepest internal needs and hungers, such as those for the warmth of friendliness, the reassurance of recognition, the feeling of importance that comes from being needed, respected, and admired.

Let us forget entirely for the moment the great benefits that flow to him, and think only of the personal gain to us of treating the other fellow like a fellow human being. In other words, let us think only of what we get out of it; of what is in it for us.

To begin with, we know that our chances for success in a job, in the leadership of people, in social life, and in the home is for all intents and purposes negligible if we have not learned the arts of being friendly, considerate, and understanding in our relationship with people.

Positively stated, this means that success in the major areas of our lives is largely the payoff to us of our good human relationships. It is money in our pockets, promotion both financial and technical on the job, and happiness in our social and home life.

We know, too, that it is only through our relationships that we can obtain the satisfactions of the deeper internal needs and hungers of our own egos, such as the need for recognition, security, and for being needed and wanted.

But fellow human beings give to us only what we give to them. Normal people pay off in kind. It is inevitable that they do so. It is an automatic response dictated by nature. Feed their internal hungers and sooner or later they will feed ours. Starve their hungers and that is what they will do to us. But it is through our relationships with people that we feed or starve them as persons, and ourselves in turn. Thus another payoff to us of good human relationship is that it draws to us the satisfactions we need to be mentally healthy and emotionally sound and harmonious.

Looking at good human relationships from the viewpoint of personal advantage, it is apparent that it is not a fringe ornament. It is a necessity of life for us. Not only is it the predominant factor in our domestic, social, and vocational success and happiness, it is the indispensable one in the unfoldment of our human personality. Without it the food needed for mental and emotional wholeness would not be given to us.

An investment of self in good human relations pays huge dividends to the self.

A PERSONAL RIGHT

For most men about one third of their time each day is put in at work making a living.

Some employer or other contracts for this time and skill with the assumption that its contribution to the business, at the very least, will be equal to the compensation given for it in the way of wage or salary.

The desirable situation, however, is the one in which the mutual relationships of the employer and employee are such that both receive more than the minimum from each other. It is one in which the spirit of loyalty transcends the idea of obligation, and reaches itself into a relationship where both employer and employee habitually strive to contribute to each other the maximum they are able to give.

It follows naturally from this that a man should not go to work for an organization if he does not have implicit faith that it will do everything in its power to make his work effective and satisfying.

On the other hand, he should not continue to accept a salary from the employer to whom he is not willing to give his best, either because he is unable to agree with the methods of management, or for some other reason cannot be loyal to the employer.

If a person cannot reconcile himself to the way his employer operates; if he must constantly be critical of how things are done; if he is generally unhappy about decisions or policies made, he ought to separate connections, and find a place of employment in which policies are consistent with his ideas and views.

It would be better for the company, and infinitely better for himself. For he is the real loser in staying where he is unhappy. His eight hours of work a day could be turned into satisfying and effective ones if they were given to a firm in which he believed, and to whom he could give his loyalty and maximum effort.

It is distinctively a privilege of our democratic way of life to be able to get out of a job that we don't like, or a firm in whose management we have no faith. It is a personal right that is to be cherished, the right to seek happiness elsewhere. But, fortunately, this is seldom necessary, for the interests of management and the other employees are, after all, one and the same, and there exists, as a rule, a mutual devotion and loyalty that is deep and unshakable.

GETTING ALONG WITH ONESELF

A fundamental factor in human relations is that the first and basic element in it is getting along with oneself.

One can know all the principles that apply to the interrelationship of people, and yet fail to make that relationship good. One can learn all the traits that tend to make human relations satisfactory and effective, and yet not succeed, if one's relationship with oneself is not in good order.

Getting along with others is in a large measure an extension of one's good relationship with oneself. It is a natural flow of one's own peace, contentment, and attitude towards life and towards those with whom one associates. Poor human relations, on the other hand, are too frequently the symptoms of our own inward unrest, tensions, and insecurity.

In other discussions we have mentioned various things that were necessary to assure good relationship within ourselves. For instance, we have mentioned the fundamental needs of man that must be satisfied, such as his need to satisfy physical stresses, his need for recognition, service, craftsmanship, and faith. We have also mentioned the activities of man that most naturally satisfied these needs. We called these "The Big Four,"—Work, Worship, Play, and Love.

We also mentioned strategies that could be used to help us remain free of the internal disorder that disturb our relationship with ourselves. One of these was Dr. Osler's philosophy of living within each twenty-four hour period.

There are, of course, many other things that one can do to

help keep one's relationship with oneself in good order. Man, through his experiences down the centuries, has learned many ways, simple and complex, of avoiding the destructive conditions of body, mind, and heart that make getting along with ourselves difficult, if not impossible.

Among the wisdom accumulated by him is the recognition of the necessity of keeping himself free of the destructive and deadly emotions, such as fear, anger, hate, greed, and jealousy.

And all of us know some of the more simple ways of thinking and of acting that help us maintain inward composure and that make it easier for us to get along with ourselves. We know, for instance, the importance of handling and solving our problems intellectually, and not emotionally; of not taking ourselves too seriously; of developing a sense of humor; and of looking at life in perspective and as a whole.

All of us know, too, that if we wish to keep our relationship with ourselves good, we must learn to accept things as they are, and must learn to find contentment and happiness in the things that are simple and that are near and close to us. We know that we must learn to seek and find what we want, not in distant and faraway utopias, but right in our own back yards.

PAY CHECK PLUS

If a man is in a job only for the pay check he gets out of it, he is cheating himself.

Somewhere there is work that he could do that would give him more than a pay check. It would give him what, in the long run, is of even greater importance—a sense of worthwhileness. It would give him a deep satisfaction in doing something that, in his belief, is important for its own sake.

A job is an integral part of a man's life—not just because it gives him the means of a livelihood. Its connection is deeper than that. A job is something in terms of which most of us cast our lives. It shapes, forms, and determines our lives for us.

It is through our job that we find expression for ourselves. It is the medium through which we make our contribution to mankind. It is the link that connects our efforts with the efforts of others to make life and progress possible for mankind. It is for most of us, too, the only way we have of putting into play the particular talents or aptitudes that distinguish us as distinct individuals and entities.

If a man then works for pay only; if he does not believe in the importance of his job; if he is not inspired by its mission as an instrument of contribution, he is indeed to be pitied. He has missed what could be the integrating force and drive of his entire life.

Such an individual should by all means get out of that job and find a work activity that has meaning to him, and one in which he believes with his whole heart and soul. Since his work

200

and his life are largely identified, he should get into the kind of job that gives to his life significance, purpose, and direction.

It makes no difference how little or how much a job pays us in money, if we do not get from it the satisfaction of doing something that to us is important, we are getting a bad bargain. We are the losers. We lose in two ways. First, we lose one of life's major and most satisfying experiences. Secondly, we lose the best of all chances for success. There is no other force that drives us so constantly and surely toward success as does belief in one's work.

HUMAN DIGNITY AND HUMAN RIGHTS

– ⚜ –

Human dignity and human or natural rights are inseparable. Because man has human dignity he has certain rights, and when he is denied the exercise of those rights, his dignity is violated.

Human dignity is not purchased through wealth. It is not obtained through power, influence, or position. It is not the result of social or political standing, or of education. It is not something peculiar to any one economic or social class, or any creed, or nationality. It is rather an inherent property or nature that is common to all men, poor or rich, skilled or unskilled, educated or illiterate, civilized or savage.

It is the mark of a human being. It is that which distinguishes him from the rest of the animals or from any other created thing. It is God-given, and became an essential part of man's nature when the Creator made him according to His own likeness.

Being made in the likeness or in the image of God means that man was given some of the attributes that are part of the nature of God. Consequently, he has intelligence, a free will, is capable of noble emotions, and is spiritually immortal. From this dignity of his nature stem certain rights which are known as natural rights and which impose an obligation both on him and on those who have any kind of relations with him.

As far as his own actions are concerned, for instance, he has the power of free will. Thus he has the moral right to make his own decisions. But he also has the obligation to exercise this right in a manner consistent with his dignity as a human being, and with full respect for the dignity and rights of other human beings. If he acts otherwise he violates not only the rights of others, but his own dignity as well.

All men have a natural right to the intelligent ordering of their own lives. They have a right to liberty, to justice, to a full compensation for their labor, to a fair and honest consideration of their grievances, to make a living, to grow within the limits of their potentiality. They have a right to be treated fairly, considerately, and honestly.

Whenever any one of these rights is not respected in our dealings with another, and this includes the minute dealings of everyday life, the intent of nature is aborted. Human relationships are disorganized and damaged. The fulfillment of a life and a personality is blocked. A serious indignity against human nature is perpetrated.

Respect for the natural rights of others in every detail of life is the only thing that will assure to every individual the realization of his highest potential life and destiny. It is, too, the essential factor in all human relations, whether these be on the job, at home, or in social, economic, or political activities. In fact, it is the key to world peace and to universal well-being.

No individual or nation, regardless of power or importance, can call itself civilized or mature unless the respect for human dignity and rights has become the basic determinant of its every action and relationship.

FROM WHOSE POINT OF VIEW?

Many of our sincerest attempts to please or motivate others fail in their objective simply because we make the effort from the point of view of what would please or motivate us.

We unconsciously assume that things that are important to us are *ipso facto* important to the other person. We take it for granted that things which would please us or be significant to us would also be so for every other human being.

Unfortunately, this is not according to fact and, consequently, often our best efforts are frustrating and disappointing. Many of us eventually give up our efforts to please since our experience convinces us that others are not receptive, that they do not appreciate our good graces towards them, or that they are plainly demanding or ungrateful.

The lack of receptiveness or of adequate appreciation, however, could be our fault. It cannot always be attributed to the insensitive or demanding nature of those whom we try to please. Our fault is that we look at others from our point of view and from the point of our observation of ourselves. In other words, we try to please them by doing what is not necessarily pleasing to them, or what may in some cases actually be offensive to them.

One of the most difficult things to understand in our relationships to others is that all people are not of the same make-up as we are. They are like us, it is true, in some basic needs that are common to all men, but as individual persons they are unlike us or anyone else. They have different tastes, different values, and different interests. Their parental inheritances, their background, their social experiences, and their education are all different. Yet it is the sum total of these that shapes each individual into the distinct person he is and that determines his tastes and values.

To please or motivate him, then, we must put ourselves into his shoes and look at things from his particular point of observation. It is his tastes, needs, values, and beliefs that we must consider. The fact that we like chocolates does not mean that he likes them. He may have developed no taste for them, or, perhaps, some unpleasant experiences with them may have made chocolates actually distasteful to him. A gift of chocolates could leave him entirely unresponsive. It could possibly, under certain conditions, annoy him.

So it is with every other act in our relationship to him. To be successful in accomplishing its motive, it must be attuned to his particular needs, desires, likes, and dislikes; and it must also be attuned to the degree of urgency in which these are a part of his nature. The greater the degree of his want and desire for something, the more will its satisfaction please him.

If, for instance, he does not like rice, we cannot expect to please him by setting a bowl of rice before him. If he has no particular urgency for security, we don't motivate him by showering him with security. If, on the other hand, he has a pressing need or hunger for recognition or for other intangibles, we influence him favorably by doing that which helps him think more highly of himself. We cannot expect to do so by feasting him with material things.

The point of it is that we cannot please or motivate the other person by giving him the things that we think he likes simply because we like them. We must do so by giving him what he likes and what is important to him from the point of view of his particular wants and hungers. We will then find that he is responsive and appreciative, and that our relationships with him will be satisfying and rewarding ones.

THAT WHICH WE THINK IMPOSSIBLE

Many of the greatest accomplishments of the human race could be written in terms of the attainments of men and women who, according to the usual norms, did not have a single chance for success.

Men and women so severely handicapped by physical or social afflictions that they could not possibly succeed in their field—it is their story, in the area of their specific handicaps, that has given mankind its greatest achievements.

Demosthenes in oratory; Columbus in navigation; Disraeli in statesmanship; Beethoven in music; Lincoln in social justice and humanitarianism; Steinmetz in experimental science; Cunningham in the mile sprint; Helen Keller in courage; George Washington Carver in the development of foods; hundreds of men and women in business and industrial leadership; a simple, humble Galilean in brotherhood and love.

Yes, it is always the same story. Men doing the impossible? No! It is men doing that which was thought to be impossible!

No one can put a square peg into around hole, it is true. But let us be sure before we call it impossible, that the peg is really square, or that it cannot be rounded out to fit.

A man without legs obviously cannot become the world's fastest sprinter. But, a man with legs, even if they seem useless, has a chance—if he believes, and, if he tries hard enough!

No! It is not the impossible that keeps us from success.

It is that which *we think* is impossible.

207

AWARENESS AND APPRECIATION

It has frequently been said by observers of human nature that the knack of being aware of his blessings and of feeling appreciation for them is a distinctive characteristic of the mature man.

Unfortunately, many of us feel very differently about our blessings. In place of recognizing them, we take them for granted. In place of feeling appreciation for the good things we have, we think largely of the blessings we do not have. As a result, we live with resentment and dissatisfaction rather than with appreciation.

The mature man, however, feels differently. He does not take his blessings for granted. He values what he has, if only for the reason, perhaps, that he does not think in terms of what he does not have, but rather in terms of what he might not have if the conditions and circumstances of his life were less favorable to him.

If he has two strong legs with which to walk, he is not unmindful of the fact that he could be one of the thousands of fellow human beings who have only one leg or none at all. When he is seated by his table with a sufficiency of nourishing food to sustain him, he does not forget that he could be one of the millions of human beings whose lot is famine and starvation. When he tucks away warmly and securely for the night the healthy little child that is his son or daughter, he is not forgetful that this child might have been one of the countless underprivileged, crippled, disease-ridden, or rejected little ones that are to be found in every nook and corner of the earth.

Nor does the mature man deceive himself into believing that there is a law of life that assures him health, a job with which to earn a living, a safe and comfortable home, a land of freedom in which to live, churches in which to worship, schools in which to educate his children, or a culture in which to grow, prosper, and fulfill himself.

He knows better, for he knows that if there were such a law of life it would have to be applicable universally. The bereaved, the sick, the crippled, the impoverished, the illiterate, the underprivileged, and the persecuted among the peoples the world over give him unquestionable testimony against such universality.

Since the mature man thus thinks maturely, he knows that whatever good things he has are blessings which need not have been made available to him. They are not solely the products of his labors. He knows that they are as much the gift of an Unseen Force that keeps Its Protective Wing folded over and around him.

Because he is aware of his blessings, the mature man appreciates them. And because he appreciates them, he finds contentment and happiness within their framework.

FIRST, AN OBJECTIVE

The most general cause for our mediocrity in performance or for our failure in accomplishment is not lack of ability. It is not unwillingness to work. It is not indifference, or a lack of sincerity.

It is rather that we do not formulate specific, concrete objectives towards which to direct our efforts. It is that we do not set specific goals for ourselves. It is that we aim our efforts at vague generalizations, and not at bull's eyes.

Ask almost any individual what he hopes to get out of life, and he will answer with the generalizations of success and happiness. Ask him to narrow down these concepts to what he specifically means, and he is at a loss for an answer. He wants success and happiness, but he has not defined them for himself into any specific terms or constituents. As a result, in his efforts to reach these he is doing no more than groping blindly in a fog, with no sense of direction nor a compass, toward an objective that he has not formulated and that he would not recognize if he reached it.

Yet, success and happiness, or for that matter, any accomplishments, are seldom, if ever, accidental. They are the end result of planned effort towards specific objectives.

First must come the objective. It must be spelled out. It must have a boundary. It must be concretely visualized. We cannot hit a mark that is not set. We cannot paint a picture of which we have no mental image. We cannot build a house according to a blueprint if we have not blueprinted it. We cannot reach a particular destination that we have not first "particularized."

So is it in all of life's activities. Successfully to achieve, we must first concretely define what we mean to do. We must translate it into objectives towards which we can directly concentrate our efforts.

If we would be, for instance, successful salesmen, we must first concretely define to ourselves what we mean by "successful salesman." What to us does it mean in terms of sales production figures? What does it mean in terms of service to our clients, of educational and training courses for greater professional proficiency, of participation in community leadership and in social and religious activity?

Would we be the more ideal persons, mothers, father, employees, teachers, or ministers? This remains a mere generalization until we have visualized what is to us that ideal and what we must become to give substance to it.

No, it is seldom our lack of interest in bettering ourselves, or our unwillingness to put in the effort necessary that is the cause of our mediocrity. It is much more often the fact that we have failed in defining for ourselves in concrete terms what we want to be or achieve. We have set for ourselves no concrete goal towards which to strive. We work honestly and sincerely, but aimlessly towards generalizations.

GOOD FOR ONE: GOOD FOR THE OTHER

—◆◊◆—

Our job is by no means our entire life. It is, however, a very important part of it. As a rule, in fact, our lives and jobs become largely identified.

One takes on the hues and colors of the other. The kind of life we live as persons largely determines the kind we live as workers. The opposite is true, too. What we are and do as workers inevitably has its effects on our lives as personal individuals.

Any effort an individual makes to raise the caliber of his personal life has a direct bearing on the success of his job life. We generally think of the elevation of one's personal life in terms of the development of finer character, better personality, more mature adjustment to life, better thinking ability, the acceptance of responsibility, more balanced sense of values, skill in seeing things as a whole and not just in isolated parts, tolerance and understanding, social rather than self-centered consciousness, and finally, the development of length and breadth in imagination and vision.

Yet, these are also predominately the things that make for greater success in one's job life. Many people have the idea that job success is essentially a matter of technical knowledge and skill. The importance of these, of course, cannot be minimized. They are fundamental. We must, however, face the fact that technological skill by itself rarely assures a high measure of job success. To concentrate on it to the point of neglecting the factors that make for stature of the entire person must end disappointingly.

Behind the skill, and inseparable from it, is the person. Skill is accepted and approved only to the degree in which the person gains approval. The same qualities that bring stature and success to the individual's personal life also bring stature and success in his job life.

If we wish to fit ourselves for success on the job, we must concentrate on those things which shape with distinction our own persons and personal lives. By all means must we develop job know-how. But on top of the foundation of skill we must build the superstructure that makes us superior as persons.

It is the standards and values that we have as individuals; it is the respect that we have for the dignity and rights of others; it is our integrity, our sense of justice, our tolerance; it is our desire to give more than we take, and our willingness to cooperate with others for the common good; it is to accept our responsibilities; it is to do what is right for right's sake. It is these qualities that bring success to work just as they do to our more personal and intimate lives.

STRANGE TEACHINGS, INDEED!

For over nineteen hundred years millions of men and women throughout the world have knelt in reverence and love before the crib of Bethlehem.

They have knelt there in quiet adoration and worship before a Child in whose simple teachings they found the way to the richness within themselves and within their lives. They found there a way of life that brought fulfillment, happiness, and peace; a way of life that brought material as well as spiritual well-being and success.

It was about themselves, and about their relationships to their neighbors and to their God that this Child taught them.

Love one another, He urged them. Try to understand your neighbor and his ways and problems. Practice justice. Be merciful. Forgive those who err. Trust the Father who is above you, and Who made you and cares for you. Believe in yourself and in your great powers. Be selfless, and all things will be given unto you.

In His teachings He spoke of meekness, gentility, tolerance, understanding, forgiveness, trust, faith, selflessness, justice, mercy, fearlessness, strength, serenity, harmony, and love.

These were strange precepts in a world bent on the idolatry of power and of materialistic selfishness. Yet these teachings worked. Men who followed them found a new world open to them. They found self-fulfillment. Their lives became satisfying and meaningful to them.

Often His teachings seemed paradoxical. If you want to find yourself, He said, you must lose yourself. You must give yourself away. If you want to receive in overflowing measures, you must give away of that which you have. If a man smite you on one cheek, turn to him the other also. Love those who hate and despise you.

Strange teachings, indeed! But stranger still is the fact that those who accepted them as a way of life found the most illusive, yet the most desired of all things of life, peace within themselves. From the Child in the crib they had learned the way to the kingdom within themselves.

REPAYMENT IN SERVICE

For the blessings of the past we are grateful.

For those we are to receive in the future we hope to make ourselves worthy and deserving.

We are deeply conscious that life is a bounteous giver, and that the blessings showered upon us are in near unlimited disproportion to those which we have a right to expect on the basis of our merit.

This disproportion makes us the debtor and imposes on us the obligation of giving as much as we can in return. It requires, in fairness and justice, that we forsake the purely receiving role of the infant, and add the giving role of the mature adult. It demands that we give back to life something that will enrich and enlarge it to take the place of what we receive from it.

To live maturely we must, among other things, pay rent for the space we occupy on earth. We must, too, add something to the stream of civilization for what countless men and women in present and past ages have fed into it for the betterment and enrichment of our lives. In brief, maturity demands that we must give back to life in return for what we receive from it.

We do this largely through the giving of ourselves in service to our fellow men. This does not mean that we must unduly deprive ourselves, nor that we devote ourselves to enterprises of great magnitude. Nor does it mean that we have to serve in the complete sense of an Albert Schweitzer. It does mean, however, that we devote ourselves to the tasks at hand, and that

216

we enlarge the focus of our attention and concentration to include the needs, problems, and hopes of the other members of our families, work groups, and communities.

To expect greatly from the future, but to be prepared also to give greatly for what we receive is the responsible and mature approach. It is the only one acceptable to the grown-up man or woman. It is not an optional way, but a required one, for the very nature of maturity is to be able to go on one's own, to earn one's keep, and to pay for what one receives. None of us can, of course, repay to life more than a fraction of what he receives from it, but the mature man recognizes his obligations, and by giving himself in service, pays his debt in as large a measure as possible.

To expect greatly from the future, but to be prepared and ready to give as greatly as possible in return for its blessings, is indeed the mature way of living.

THE PEACE OF BETHLEHEM

Men of wisdom have universally taught that man to have peace of mind and heart must first get himself "off his hands."

He must reach outward and away from himself into the lives of other people. He must lose himself in a cause, in an inspired accomplishment, or in some other form of selfless service.

Satisfaction of mind or peace of heart can never be obtained in self-directed activity. Man must look out for himself, it is true, but he can never find fulfillment of self, until his thoughts and actions have been focused on the well-being and happiness of others.

"Give and it shall be given unto you," "Lose yourself and you shall find yourself" were fundamental precepts in the teaching of the Child whose birthday we commemorate on Christmas Day.

Unwittingly man proves to himself each year during the Season of Christmas the truth of these great precepts of self-lessness. At least for one day his whole self is filled with what is often called the peace of Bethlehem. "Why?" we ask. The answer is simple. It is because for this one day he loses himself and becomes completely wrapped up in the desire to bring joy to someone outside of himself.

He becomes, if you wish, a Santa Claus, whose only purpose is to give joy and happiness to a child, a friend, or a loved one. He gives a little of himself or his goods to bring cheer and greater well-being to the poor, the sick, the bereaved, the hapless, and the lonely. For one short day he loses sight of himself to bring peace and good will to his fellow men on earth.

As a result the wonderful miracle happens. He discovers the kingdom within himself. The conflicts, tensions, and uncertainties that beset him dissolve, and in their place his heart glows with peace, security, and joy.

He has lived for one day, as he was meant to live each day, that is, outside of himself. He has, perhaps, unconsciously, put to work in his life one of the greatest of all mental and spiritual laws, that to find himself, he must first lose himself in selflessness and love.

He has found the peace of Bethlehem.

BEARING GENTLY WITH OUR FELLOW MEN

One indication of personal maturity is a man's readiness to accept other people as they are, and not to allow himself to be irritated or offended by them.

The immature individual often does not accept graciously any manners or ways of life that are different from his. Hence he is easily irritated or offended with others who have different beliefs, customs, or personality patterns. To him any ways of talking, thinking, and acting that are not in conformity with his own are objectionable.

Similarly inclined to be intolerant of the ways of others is the individual who, because of the frustration of his life, is filled with pent-up inward hostility. He is quick at taking offense and at giving tactless expression to his irritation. As a result, his relationships with others are frequently strained. He is rejected by his associates, and pays the penalty in loss of social and business success.

In the development of an effective social or business personality it is necessary that we guard ourselves against the forming of this habit of taking offense at the behavior of others.

This, of course, is not easy. Man as such has many different customs, beliefs, prejudices, and degrees of maturity and immaturity. He, too, has many weaknesses. Sometimes he is ignorant. Often he is deeply prejudiced. Frequently he is hostile in his behavior. Sometimes he is downright mean. To adjust ourselves to these differences and to accept them requires understanding and empathy.

Nevertheless, if we wish our relationships with man to be good it is important that we form the habit of bending with him as the branch of the tree bends with the wind to absorb its shock. We must learn not to take offense, but to bear with him gently, just as we wish he would bear with us in our own immaturities.

In his *Meditations* the emperor and philosopher Marcus Aurelius states a thought pertaining to this. The great Stoic writes: "For it is in no way right to be offended with men, but it is thy duty to care for them and to bear with them gently."

This takes self-discipline and maturity. However, I can think of few things that would be more valuable in our social and business relations than to learn not to take offense at others, and to bear gently with our fellow men.

FUNCTIONAL OR VESTIGIAL?

Our thinking as a rule is more often negative than positive.

We think of the possibilities of defeat more frequently than we do of the certainty of success.

Rather than reach for the stars knowing that our reach will stretch, we fear to reach lest it fall short of its mark.

Since it is not possible to separate our thoughts from our deeds, such negative thinking largely explains our mediocrity and defeat in daily performance. The thought is the father of the deed, and as we think so we do. To channel our energies into greater accomplishments we need to get control of our minds and of our belief in ourselves. We need to re-appraise our potentialities to do.

We cannot help wondering what has happened to our self-confidence and self-reliance; our courage to pioneer and to take on new adventures. What has happened to our faith in ourselves and to our fortitude to stick with an endeavor until we have successfully accomplished it? Why are we willing to stay in a groove simply because getting out of it means some positive thinking and positive effort? Why are we willing to accept the crumbs from the table in place of the fruits of life, rather than snap out of the defeatism of our negative thinking?

Has our thinking become so wishy-washy that we can no longer face ourselves with faith and confidence? Has it become so negative that we must stick our heads in the sand to avoid seeing what we do not have the courage to face?

222

Probably one of the most important decisions that each of us has to make for himself is whether his faculties to dream, to plan, to create, and to believe are functional or vestigial. Have the powers of our ancient heritage to be in command of our lives been fossilized? Have they lost their utility? If that consciously or unconsciously is our thinking we are mere puppets of fate. In that event individual efforts are a waste of time.

If, on the other hand, we believe our powers and faculties to be functional; if we accept the fact that we have the powers to dream, to plan, to create, and to believe, we ought to start using them positively to take command of the small and large affairs of our daily lives. Each of us would then be the master of his destiny.

THE NURSERY OR REALITY

One of our great writers has stated if we need to be tucked away in our nursery beds each night with the assurance that all is right with the world, we are not ready to leave that nursery to face life on our own. We have not yet learned to face reality.

Life is not *all* right. It never was, and it never will be, and the sooner we learn that fact, the sooner will we be able to live it effectively and happily. Life is not a nursery tale with a happy ending for each chapter. It is rather a story loaded heavily with difficulties, problems, obstacles, and frustrations; and with many of them insurmountable.

This does not mean that life is largely unfriendly or hostile to us. The fact is that it is predominately good. But the belief that the complicated and innumerable forces that make up life will never in their interrelationships be opposed to our personal plans and interests is unrealistic.

To become aware of that fact and to accept it is one of the first steps towards successful and happy living. To expect problems and frustrations as natural and inevitable is to be prepared for them and to take them in stride, just as we do the favorable and beneficent aspects of life.

Too many of us live in the childish fantasy that life is meant to be a bed of roses without thorns. When something happens that affects us adversely, our personal little universe is to us abused and threatened. With excessive self-concern and self-pity we respond to the threat with emotional stewing about it.

Problems to us are isolated and unnatural things and are ominous in nature.

When, on the other hand, we have grown sufficiently to look at life with an adult sense of reality, we expect these problems just as we expect to become hungry or thirsty. We meet them head on and do something about them. We apply intellectual processes to their solutions. Gradually we learn that problems often have positive human values. It is through them that we grow and become seasoned. It is in overcoming them that we gain self-reliance and self-confidence. It is in accepting those that we cannot solve, such as the death of a loved one, that we learn one of life's most valued skills—that of adapting and adjusting ourselves to what we cannot change.

The amazing thing, however, is that so many of us persist in the expectation of living without opposition or struggle. There is no justification anywhere in the nature of things or in the experiences of mankind for such an illusion. Nor would man want such an existence. What weaklings we would soon become if we could remain forever in the sheltered security of our mother's breast.

If to feel safe and secure we need the assurance that life has no problems or frustrations, we had better return to our nursery with its fairy tales. If, on the other hand, we expect obstacles and tribulations as part of the warp and woof of life; if we are prepared to accept them and to cope with them just as we do with other natural phenomena such as our hungers and thirsts, we are facing reality. We are then ready to leave the nursery and take charge of our lives. We have grown into adulthood.

EXTENSION OR ATROPHY?

To live completely a man must seek extension of himself in some other facets of life than in the things that pertain merely to his own particular well-being.

To live only within the niche of his own self-interest is to lay waste his unique power of multiplying himself and of taking personal part simultaneously in various activities that challenge the interest of mature members of society.

And it can be said without qualifications that no human being can consider himself mature if he narrows the use of his efforts, talents, or means to his own personal advantage. The very concept of maturity rests on the degree of inner growth that is characterized by a yearning within the individual to transcend his self-concentration by extending himself into the lives of others. In other words, maturity is a stage in his development, when to live with himself in a satisfying manner it becomes imperative for him to give as well as to receive.

Maturing is an inward force to extend and multiply himself. Its analogy in the world of nature is that "vital something" that makes the tree bear fruit. The presence of this force in man does not mean, however, that he always recognizes it as such. He may be deeply aware of a striving within himself, or perhaps a voidness that he seeks to fill, and yet may not pinpoint it as the inner need to extend and multiply himself. In many other instances, man identifies it, but has not learned the ways of giving himself, or of becoming aware of the opportunities in his surroundings for such self-extension.

226

Man must, however, find extension and multiplication of himself, or resign himself to the inevitable fate of a dwarfed and anemic life. He must "bear fruit" and multiply himself in facets of life other than those which concern him alone.

Unconsciously he does this through his devotion to his loved ones. But beyond this, he needs consciously to make himself a part of the activities of the larger social group: his community, the nation, even the world at large.

The most effective way of doing this, although limited in extension, is through giving of himself by way of his time, effort, and talents to the various social, civic, educational, charitable, and religious projects of his community. "It is" in the words of Kahlil Gibran in *The Prophet*, "when you give of yourself that you truly give."

Another way is by the giving of himself through his means. This method makes possible his participation regardless of time, distance, personal affairs, or of any special skills and disciplines needed in the devotion or task.

A few pennies given to the polio fund takes him in service to the Rehabilitation Centers for crippled children; a few pennies to the Church enlarges him into a spiritual missionary; a few pennies to an educational institution actively places him in a classroom developing the minds and hearts of the young.

He can thus through his means extend himself into simultaneous participation in the cancer research laboratories, in the homes of the poor and afflicted, in the civic endeavors of his community, or in the struggles for liberty and dignity by the peoples of faraway nations whose names or geographical locations may be unknown to him.

In this matter of living for himself or of enlarging himself man has really only one alternative: extension or atrophy.

THE SECRET: TO WANT IT BADLY ENOUGH

Ultimately, the question of what we get out of life resolves itself into what we want badly enough from it.

In the last analysis, there is really only one secret to success. It is to know specifically what we want and to want it so much that we are willing to pay whatever the price to obtain it.

The important factor leading to success is rarely that of time, means, or of ability. It is rather the inward drive or motive that gets us to use our means, ability, and time in their full potential towards the reaching of a specific objective. The one motive that will put our powers fully to work to attain an objective is to want it badly enough. It is to get sufficiently hungry for something so that obtaining it becomes the paramount issue in our lives.

The principle involved is one of common experience in our minor daily affairs. Consider the financial aspects, for instance. How often we cannot afford a dollar for a prosaic new broom, but we can somehow or other get a hundred dollars for a new golf set, or three thousand of them for a new car. This applies also to the availability and expenditure of our time, energy, and ability. Somehow or other we find a surplus of these if we really want something badly enough.

The same is true of the larger things of life. We find few impregnable barriers between us and what we want with all our hearts and minds. First, however, we must know specifically what we really want. Most of us do not. Ask any one hundred thousand men what they want most of all to accomplish in their lives, or even in the present day, and very few can give anything but a nebulous generalization.

Unfortunately we cannot fall in love sufficiently with a generalization to want it badly enough to pay any demanded price for it. It takes a specific objective to make us burn with so deep a desire. If, on the other hand, we focus the objective and wish it with enough hunger or desire, we will stop at no obstacles. We will recognize no impossibility.

If we check the lives and struggles of those who have risen to leadership in statesmanship, art, business, industry, philosophy, religion, medicine, law, science, engineering, or any other human endeavor, we will find a common denominator. More often than not we will find men and women of a humble and lowly origin and background who had nothing to start with nor to sustain them in their struggles except a specific dream and the deep desire or hunger to give substance to it.

The wellspring of those who have excelled in attaining happiness, or in doing their jobs superbly: the woman preeminent as a wife and mother; the priest in his church; the shoemaker at his bench; or a president in the White House at Washington, is that they wanted badly enough to become what they are to pay the price demanded. No aimless wandering, nor silver spoons in their mouths at the time of birth, made them what they became.

To know what we want and to want it badly enough recognizes no obstacles or impossibilities. It is the wellspring of human determination and drive. It is the one secret to success. All other needed factors follow as a matter of course in its wake.

BETTERING OUR HUMAN RELATIONSHIPS

In human relations we get back as a whole the kind of relations we give.

We reap the harvest of what we sow and plant.

The mill of human relations feeds back to us the behavior with which we relate or communicate ourselves to the other person.

Friendliness brings back friendliness. Helpfulness returns in helpfulness. Understanding breeds and nourishes understanding. Love returns in love, justice in justice, good will in good will.

But so does hostility bring back hostility. Anger returns in anger; pettiness, in pettiness. Unfriendliness draws unfriendliness; inconsiderateness invites inconsiderateness; selfishness draws selfishness.

Certainly there are many exceptions to this general principle. This is particularly so when frequently our finest social efforts are met with negative responses. Unfortunately in dealing with human beings we come across those of pronounced emotional immaturity and those of deep emotional hostilities. These individuals tend to respond not in kind, but in terms of their own attitudes.

As a rule, however, we get back from others in kind the behavior through which we relate ourselves to them. And it is our failure to live according to this basic principle that is the root of many of our most tragic mistakes in our relationships with others. Not only do we neglect to give to the other person the kind of relationship we would like to have back from him; but what is, perhaps, worse is that we react toward his bad behavior in terms of that bad behavior. We return slights to our ego with slights to the other fellow's ego. We fight anger with anger, selfishness with selfishness, hostile aggressiveness with vindictiveness. We tend to get even with the other person by returning injury for what he has done to injure us.

The result is that we increase and multiply the very thing that is most destructive to our good human relationships. We mushroom and intensify it. We give back what we receive, and in return get more of it. And so the vicious circle perpetuates and enlarges itself.

The implication is that we could improve our human relationships considerably by following the simple principle of giving to the other person in our relationships with him only what we would like him to give back to us. This applies even when we are provoked by his behavior to return blow for blow. I know of no other principle of behavior that in the long run pays greater dividends in better human relationships.

AS A MAN THINKETH

"A man can only rise, conquer, and achieve by lifting up his thoughts. He can only remain weak, and abject, and miserable by refusing to lift up his thought."

These well-known words come from a famous book *As A Man Thinketh* by James Allen, written at the beginning of the present century. It was one of the first of the best modern books to show the influence of thought in the shaping of the individual man or woman.

Today it is a commonplace belief that man is the product of his own thinking, and that he is the potter who takes himself which is the clay, and through the potter's wheel which are his thoughts, molds and shapes himself and his life into any design he wishes—good or bad, beautiful or ugly.

We are convinced now that if we harbor certain kinds of thoughts long enough, we will become an embodiment of them, and that we can debase or elevate our lives by the thoughts we think and cherish.

We believe that thinking success, makes success; thinking failure, makes failure; and that if a man wishes his life to be constructive, he must think constructive and positive thoughts.

Even his environment is the reflection of his thoughts. One man hears the rain on his roof, and he complains about the wetness and humidity of the day. The other man exclaims with joy about the benefits to his garden and fields that come in its wake.

To one person an evening at home is a time of inactivity and boredom; to another it is a succession of pleasant and joyful moments with loved ones. To one person his job is a necessary evil to earn the means of existence; to another it is a daily period of creativeness and challenge, invigorating and satisfying.

But the point is that it is all a matter of thinking. It is his thoughts that shape man, his environment, and his life, and that make them what they are. And it follows, that to change the nature of one's character, or the course of one's life, one must feed into the stream of his thoughts what one wishes himself and his life to become.

I believe with the poet, that

"Mind is the Master power that moulds and makes,
And Man is Mind, and evermore he takes
The tool of Thought, and, shaping what he wills,
Brings forth a thousand joys, a thousand ills;
He thinks in secret, and it comes to pass;
Environment is but his looking-glass."

HANDLING ONE'S OWN PROBLEMS

One of the tests of the maturity of a man is his readiness to face problems and to do something about them himself. Maturity among other things means that a person is self-reliant, and that he is ready and able to act independently in the conduct of his life.

Anyone, of course, unless he is decidedly immature, can do a reasonably good job of so acting as long as his life flows along on an even keel, and as long as no obstacles arise to disturb or hinder its normal progression.

It is, however, when something comes along that disrupts the status quo, or that blocks the path to which we are accustomed in the quest of our objectives, or that threatens our security, that the real test of our maturity is made.

For instance, will we have the courage to admit the existence of the problem or obstacle? Will we like adult people accept responsibility for its solution, or will we like children evade the responsibility either by doing nothing about it, or by passing the buck to others for its handling? Will we, in the event that there is no way of overcoming the problem, find a way around it, or if necessary establish a new objective and adjust ourselves to it?

The mature individual is one who is flexible so that he can adapt himself to changes and circumstances over which he has no control. When established ways to his objectives are closed, he finds new ways to gain his ends. He will first try to remove the obstacles that obstruct his path, but if that fails, he will find ways or means of going around the obstacles. It is only as a last resort that the mature man will give up his objectives. If that happens, and happen it will sometimes since some problems or obstacles are insurmountable, he will find new objectives and adjust himself to them.

The mature person will never attempt, however, an escape from his problems by throwing their burden onto other shoulders. He may seek the counsel of others, but as an independent and self-reliant individual he will assume personal responsibility, and will take the initiative to follow whatever course of action the situation calls for. His problems are his, and he handles them himself.

TODAY IS LIFE

All of us would get a great deal more out of life if we started to live it, in place of putting living off until some more auspicious time.

Almost universally we have the habit of delaying what we consider to be full living until another day when we believe circumstances and conditions will be more favorable, or when present obstacles have been removed or overcome.

Our reasoning in putting it off goes somewhat like the following. When we are in high school or college, we cannot really get down to the business of living, because one important requisite for it is to graduate from school. As graduates, however, we again delay, because a job and income have become the new requisite. Having secured that, we must again delay since we cannot really live well without a mate. And then it is the setting up of a household, the rearing of the children, the putting them through college, and one thing after another until we ultimately postpone living to the period of retirement. But retirement, too, has its complications which cause further delay. Before we know it, it is too late. The end of life has arrived, but we have not yet begun the process of living.

It is always tomorrow, or at sometime in the future that we are really going to do our very best, and be our best selves. It is when some present condition has been changed; when we have more money, more leisure, more experience, more prestige; or it is when we have an office, after we are married, when the children have grown up; it is then that we will do that which we want most to do and which will give expression to our greatest powers.

It is then that we are going to give our utmost to the job each day. It is then that we will set aside a little time daily for self-improvement through reading and studying. It is then that we will affiliate with a church; that we will become active members of this or that social or civic organization; that we will become closer companions to our children; that we will give of our time and money to the service of others. It is then that we will do the many things that will win for us the friendship, respect, and love of those with whom our lives are spent.

But what a tragic mistake this is! What a sad delusion to hope to do in the future that which we think we cannot do today. The truth is that there is no tomorrow. As Doctor William Osler has pointed out, "The future is today." Today is the span of a man's life. It is pure presumption to include tomorrow, or the next day, or the next. What a man wishes with certainty to do, he has to do now — today. And if he should have a tomorrow, its measure of effectiveness will be the result of how completely he accomplished the fullness of his life in the day which has then become a yesterday.

There is only one time to do one's best, and that is now, right at this moment. All the effectiveness and fullness of life that we hope to get must be obtained at this particular moment. We must do, and live, and enjoy, and be our best now — not tomorrow or next year.

Arnold Bennett, in one of his essays, summarizes well this philosophy of living. He writes: "This that you are living now is life itself — it is much more life itself than that which you will be living twenty years hence. Grasp that truth. Dwell on it. Absorb it."

WE HURT OURSELVES

Man's greatest enemy is he himself. It is he who by his own thoughts and deeds most frequently hurts or even destroys himself.

His physical health is largely a matter of how he takes care of his body. His mental life is largely the result of what thoughts he permits himself to think. His emotional stability is the reflection of his reactions to the daily routine and vicissitudes of life. His successes in his domestic, social, and economic or work life are an expression of how he plays the game — whether he plays it according to the rules, or tries to go contrary to them. His happiness or unhappiness is the total result.

The roads that lead to health, success, and happiness are quite clearly marked. Billions of men and women have passed through life as the fore-runners and pioneers. They have left a heritage of knowledge and wisdom of what is good and fulfilling, and of that which is harmful and destructive.

We and the average human beings with whom we associate adhere to the larger precepts of correct living. We seldom radically depart from that which is basically the correct way as experienced by those who preceded us.

Yet, a tragic thing of universal experience is that most of us have a tendency to hurt and sometimes to destroy ourselves because we have permitted one, and frequently a comparatively insignificant weakness, to become dominant in our lives, or in our ways of thinking or acting.

Hamlet, a noble character, goes to his death because he is a procrastinator. The warlike and heroic Othello puts a sword in his breast because he is afflicted with jealousy. King Lear dies in poverty and broken-hearted because of an inordinate love for his offsprings.

John Bloe, honest and efficient, who worked at the next desk for the last year, has been relieved because he antagonized his fellow employees with his rudeness and lack of tact. The pretty Mary Jones is avoided by suitors because her only interest in life is in herself. The rich and accomplished Mrs. Smith is outcast socially because she struts her superiority. Jim Blake, the much liked and talented salesman, remains in the low production group or is forced out of the business because he does not budget his time to call on the required number of people each day.

And so it goes on and on. We hurt ourselves mostly by some single deficiency which in itself is usually quite minor in nature, but which nevertheless blocks the flow of our personality and of our effectiveness. It is generally something that can easily be corrected, if we become aware of it and then try to do something about it.

GIVE OTHERS THE INDISPENSABLE

There are few things more important to us human beings than being considered important.

All of us like to have acknowledgement made of the things that are of consequence to us. We want others to notice and to express interest in the possessions and accomplishments on which we pride ourselves. We want approval of whatever in our thinking is important to us, whether it is a flower bed that we have cultivated, a child of whose accomplishments we are proud, a picture that we have selected to hang over our fireplace, or a feat of intellectual acumen or of great courage.

We want anything that means something to us personally to mean something to the other person also. Deep in our hearts, although we may be unconscious of its presence, there is a want to have the other fellow place a positive value on that in which we think we excel.

What is more, we want him to express this valuation to us in words. It is not enough for us to know that he thinks well. It is so very important to us that we need to have him say it in words. Even the most worthy of our accomplishments remain insipid to us if we do not have the expressed approval of others stamped upon them.

It is an enviable personality accomplishment to develop this subtle technique of giving to others the approval they desire for whatever in their thinking is important to them. This giving of approval must not be limited to the accomplishments that come up to the standard of the particular measurements that we have set in our own minds. The measurement must frequently be in terms of the thinking and the potential talents of the individual involved.

For instance, we do not withhold approval from the child because his first crude attempt in the use of crayons does not produce the finished product of our learned techniques. Nor do we fail to admire the simple flower bed of the home gardener because it does not measure up to the artistic creation of the trained landscape artist.

We praise him, rather, because what he has done means something or is important to him as an individual. Or again, in some instances we do so because his accomplishment is in line with what can be expected from one of his age, experience, training, or background. It is obvious that if we measure all things in relationship to perfection, there would never be an occasion for the giving of approval or recognition. We would then withhold our congratulations from the youngster finishing grade school simply because he was not being graduated from high school. By the same token we would not give recognition to the college graduate because he had not acquired all the world's knowledge and wisdom.

It is this approval by others, or let us call it ego satisfaction, that is perhaps the prime force that keeps men constantly striving to better themselves. He, who through sincere approval, helps others obtain a larger measure of it is certain to be compensated with their friendship, cooperation, and loyalty. They will gather about him and work for his cause for from him they receive what is indispensable to them.

WHAT SIZE THE PACKAGE?

It is a common experience among men that we "I" ourselves to death.

We are constantly thinking in terms of ourselves. Our almost exclusive concern is for our own little selves. It is our aches, pains, progress, health, and happiness that obsess our minds and motivate our conduct.

As a result of this, very few of us ever have a reasonable amount of success or happiness. Even our health suffers and deteriorates to a condition which is below the minimum necessary for "alive" living.

Man, it is true, is so made that his first interest is his survival. As a result he has certain ego tendencies which guard against the extinction of himself. These instincts are perhaps the most basic and the strongest of his being. But even these have a group purpose which is to protect his race from extinction.

If he wishes, however, to fulfill his own being and life whose existence he thus safeguards, he is forced by the composition of his nature to give full play to a super structure of drives that are social and not egocentric in nature.

In other words, if he wishes to develop into the stature of a man, and if he wishes his life to develop up to the expectation of his Designer and Creator, he must become essentially a social being. His thoughts, feelings, and actions must be directed toward the other person. It is the only possible way for him to find personal happiness and real individual success. Even the success of his everyday business undertakings ultimately depend on how far he has been able to make himself other-people minded.

One of the wise men has said that he indeed remains a small package whose life has been directed and motivated in terms of himself. In the light of the advanced knowledge of the Mid-twentieth Century, we can say that he not only remains a small package, but also one that is frustrated in mind and heart, and sick in body. Scientific evidence has piled up to show that inward tensions are primarily the result of too much concentration on self, and that prominent among the causes of heart disease, and ulcers, and other killers of the body is man's perpetual concern about his own insignificant self.

To be whole and sound in our thoughts, and feelings, and bodies, and to be successful in our personal and occupational lives, we must learn this most important of the lessons of the ages. It is that man wrapped in himself withers and dies. It is also that only he who loses himself in his contributions to the lives of others, ultimately finds himself, and grows, prospers, and fulfills the almost unbelievable possibilities of his nature. He it is who becomes a big package.

FAITH IN OURSELVES

At the basis of every human accomplishment, be it ever so small or so large, is someone's belief in his ability to do the particular thing desired.

It is faith in ourselves, in our distinctive individuality, in our power to do what we dream of; it is faith in our innate greatness that is the spur that urges us on to effort and accomplishment. It is the force that drives us to giving form and substance to our hopes, dreams, and visions.

The wise teachers of man throughout the centuries have insisted that one of man's greatest limitations is his lack of belief in his ability to do. The experiences of mankind have confirmed that, without this faith, man can accomplish little; that without it he remains small in stature and ineffective in his powers to accomplish.

But these great teachers and men of wisdom have also insisted that there is little that man cannot accomplish if his faith in himself is sufficiently great. They have repeatedly affirmed, too, that man can develop this belief in himself, and that he can use it in his everyday existence to make of himself and his life just about anything that he wants to.

In other words, man has within him undreamed-of power and ability which he can release if he believes sufficiently in himself to set in motion, and keep in motion, the activities that are necessary to accomplish the end or purpose he has in mind.

This does not mean, of course, that he will always be effective by merely doing what he thinks will accomplish his purpose. He must keep on doing. If he does not succeed at first, he must keep on trying. Perhaps he must change his course of action. Failure must not daunt him. He must try and try again. He must keep on working, and, above all, he must keep on believing that he has the ability to succeed. Nothing will stop him who really believes in himself. He knows that he will succeed, and he will!

Nowhere is the lesson of the power of faith more simply and beautifully expressed than in the words to his disciples by the Founder of Christianity, "If Ye had faith as a grain of mustard seed, Ye might say unto this sycamine tree, Be Thou plucked up by the root, and be Thou planted in the sea; and it should obey you."

CHANGING THE BALANCE

One of the most common handicaps to highly effective living is, paradoxically, the nearly universal desire we have to do our share.

We insist on doing our share. It is part of our culture and our way of life. We want to do our bit; and there are few things that we resent more deeply than the implication that we are not doing so.

But in this idea lies the fallacy that is responsible for much mediocre or even at times ineffective living. Contributing our part, or doing our share is, at best, merely a return to the stream of life of what we have taken out of it. We take a share; we give a share in return. Nothing has been taken away or added. The balance remains the same.

But that is not enough. What is needed for fully effective living is that we change the balance. It is to put a little more in than we take out. It is to change the static condition that results from a 50-50 basis of give and take, to the more fluid one of a 51-49 basis. It is to raise the level of the stream of life by putting more into it than we take out of it, so that everyone, including ourselves, in return has a greater quantity to draw from.

It is not to be fair that counts most; it is rather to be a little more than fair in our dealings with men. It is not to do our share of work; it is to do an extra share of it. It is not to return the love that is given us, but to return it with an extra measure.

It is not to give back the friendliness, justice, kindness, cooperation, and devotion that we receive, but to give it back with a portion of dividends.

This is also true of our work, our play, and of our family relationships. It is the extra effort we put in our work that gives us recognition and advancement. It is the extra fraction of an inch that wins for us the championship in the pole vault, the broad jump, or the mile dash. It is the love we give that is in the margin beyond what we receive, that makes our hearths glow with the warmth of happiness and peace. Even in our prayers, it is the little extra fervor and earnestness that opens the ears of Heaven.

It is, then, not what we do or give, but rather that part which is beyond the expected or required that brings fullness to our lives. It is that portion which we return that is in addition to our 50-50 share; the little extra by way of interest that we add to the stream from which we draw, and of which we are a part.

ANCIENT WISDOM

It is related in the Talmud that an aged rabbi, when asked how he had merited to live so long, gave as the first of the three reasons, that he had never tried to elevate himself at the expense of his neighbors.

Thus from ancient times comes to us a statement that contains an essential principle of successful living. It is a truth that millions of people have ignored and, consequently, have found themselves disappointed and frustrated in their efforts toward success and happiness.

This great truth has within it two demonstrated and proved principles. The first is that man cannot gain high success at the expense of others. The second is that success is always the end-result of what we have done to help others to gain growth and stature and better lives for themselves.

The prevalent fallacy in the thinking of many people is that the way to success is to rise above others. Usually in our minds this means that we must keep the other fellow down. It means that we must not let him get into a condition or situation that would bring him nearer to that of our own, or least of all to one that would exalt him. It is safer, we think, to keep him where he cannot compete with or excel us.

The actual demonstrated truth is that the opposite course of thinking and action is the way to success. Success is generally considered in our culture as a matter of going places in life. It is a matter of wealth, position, and recognized leadership.

These are not the things, however, that we can obtain or

hold irrespective of other people. Their nature is such that they must be given or ceded to us by others. Their possession implies cooperation from those outside of ourselves.

This cooperation in the obtainment of our purposes we get best from those who in their hearts want us to succeed because we have helped them to gain greater stature, to satisfy their need "to count," and generally to make a better job out of their own lives.

Man has an invariable tendency to elevate above himself those who have helped him to grow and to satisfy his own innate human needs. He has an equally invariable tendency, if not a fierce determination to obstruct and defeat those who keep him down or who frustrate his efforts to realize himself.

Elevating oneself then at the expense of others is conducive neither to longevity, nor to success in business or in life.

TO OUR OWN GREATER INTEREST

One of the most helpful secrets of getting along more pleasantly and effectively in life is consciously to develop the habit of seeing the good in other people and of relating ourselves to them in terms of their better qualities.

To see the good, and to make it the basis of our relationship with the other person is not only the fair way of dealing with him, but is the most profitable to our own interest.

Unfortunate is our human tendency to see the worst in the other person, to judge him as a whole person by this deficiency and then to relate ourselves to him on the basis of that judgment. Thus we do not deal with the better part of the person— the real person. We deal only with what we dislike in him.

Nor do we in that event deal with him in terms of the real persons we are. In place of being warm, friendly, trusting, and cooperative as we are with those whom we like, we are cold, hostile, suspicious, and competitive. In our minds we are dealing with an evil, and not with a fellow human being. Our actions correspond to our mental attitude.

Unfortunately, we are often more than usually sensitive to the weaknesses and deficiencies of those we love; of those who are in competition with us in our struggle for social prestige, job promotion, salary, and recognition; and of those who are our superiors on our jobs.

In our relationships with our superiors, for instance, this sensitiveness can easily destroy our effectiveness. In place of giving our fullest cooperation to them on the basis of their good qualities, we become critical because of some deficiency or weakness, and, as a consequence, relate ourselves to them in terms of their weakness. We become blind to their strengths and virtues, and see in them only the embodiment of the deficiency. It is only too obvious that the relationships that result from such blindness sooner or later defeat us.

It is from the good in man that we profit. It is by consciously developing the habit of seeing that good and by working with it that we bring out the best that is in him for whatever purposes there is need. This is both to his advantage and to our advantage. But, and this is of greatest importance to all of us, it is only through awareness of what is good in him that we can understand the real person he is and can thus relate ourselves to him as the real persons we are.

THE TREE IN THE FOREST

Since World War II particularly, we have become increasingly indoctrinated with the idea of world consciousness. We have become acutely aware that in a world of which all points can now be reached in a few hours time, we have a responsibility that goes beyond our own nation.

We have developed a deep sense of the brotherhood of man, and a feeling of responsibility for the welfare of all nations and all peoples.

And this is as it should be. For the human race is one, and regardless of where man lives he should have the right to share in the material and cultural riches of the other. His problems, too, should be the concern of all men.

We wonder, however, if in this constant emphasis on the development and welfare of the whole world, we have not lost sight of one of its most vital aspects. Have we perhaps become so conscious of the good of the whole that we have forgotten about the individual unit that is its nucleus? In our solicitude about the forest, have we overlooked the tree?

Have we by any chance forgotten the ancient teaching, namely, that the world is made up of continents; the continents, of nations; the nations, of states; the states, of communities; the communities, of familes; and that what the whole world will be, will depend upon what the smallest unit, the family, is?

We believe that the time has come when, without losing our consciousness of the whole, we return once more to a greater awareness of the nature and development of the family and home.

It is the family unit that is the essential stuff of which the world is made. It is here that communities, and states, and nations, and continents are born, and molded, and nurtured. It is in the family that the brotherhood of man is cradled and nursed into maturity. It is here that the welfare of the world is secured.

It is the love, and peace, and security, and beauty, and culture that are found in the individual family or home, that will permeate its larger counterpart, the world. It is the ideals that are enshrined here in the hearts of its individual members, that will ultimately be enshrined in the hearts of all men the world over.

AGAINST OUR OWN BEST INTERESTS

—◦◦⧉◦◦—

Some of us seem to have a tendency to hurt ourselves. Consciously or unconsciously we persist in doing, saying, and thinking the things that are against our own best interest.

In place of going along with the stream of life, we go against it. Rather than doing the things that are known to bring success and happiness, we take the opposite course of action. Rather than entertaining the thoughts and feelings that make for a wholesome and integrated personal life, we harbor those that disturb inward tranquility and fill our lives with tensions and needless conflicts.

All of us know, for instance, that our welfare and success depends largely on the favorable reaction to us of the people with whom we associate. We know that we need their cooperation, and their willingness to help us obtain our objectives.

We know also that to get this "feeling of others" toward us, we must be friendly, considerate, understanding, and selfless in our relationship with them. We know that to motivate others to help us obtain the things we want, we must first give to them the things tangible and intangible that they need and wish as persons and as human beings.

In spite of this knowledge, we are indifferent to people. We make no effort to win their affection and good will. Many times we are hostile to them. We say unpleasant things. We belittle them. We make them lose face. We deny them the recognition they crave. Or we are contentious with them about little things that have no significance. We show off our feigned superiority of knowledge or position. We refuse to give them the chances to better or improve themselves. And all the while we are hurting ourselves more than we are them.

And so, too, in our thoughts and feelings, we allow the negative and frequently destructive ones to take over our minds and hearts. In place of thoughts of success and happiness, we think of failure and defeat. We let envy build up resentment in us toward others. We permit fear to incapacitate us. We let hate, anger, and selfishness take possession of us and debase our relationship with our fellow workers, friends, and family members.

So even in our innermost minds we are hurting ourselves, when all the while we could be entertaining thoughts and emotions that build strength, tranquility, and confidence. Instead of destroying our powers through what is negative and hostile, we could be creating our success and happiness through thoughts and emotions of courage, of faith, of sympathy, of selflessness, of understanding, of tolerance, of willingness to share, and of love.

It is strange, indeed, that some of us seem to want to do the things that are against our own best interest.

SMALL OR BIG — OUR CHOICE

Most of us human beings are seriously handicapped by our negative thinking.

We think and visualize difficulty, mediocrity, defeat, and failure. As a consequence, our lives are circumscribed by these.

We think of and visualize pennies, in place of dollars. We visualize getting by, in place of excelling. We think of ourselves as following, rather than as leading.

Our thoughts and dreams are confined to the necessities of food, shelter, and clothing. We do not think in terms of comfort and elegance. Our job goals and sales quotas, because we think in terms of smallness, are insignificant in relation to our potential. Our whole lives are the embodiment of the negativeness and defeatism of our minds.

Modern research into human accomplishment has shown that we tend strongly to become what our minds think and visualize. If we consistently think small thoughts, our lives will necessarily remain small. If we think mediocrity and defeat, that is what we reap. If we think and visualize power, confidence, success, and happiness, these will characterize our lives.

It must be remembered that we are not made up of separate entities such as of body and of mind. Nor are body and mind appended to each other. They are not elements, but rather constituents which in assimilation equal or spell out the human being.

When the mind acts, the body acts, and conversely; for it

is the living person who is acting. The most insignificant thought affects the body and the whole person just as a physical condition such as hunger, or a physical pain, changes the quality of our thoughts. Body and mind are one and of the same parcel which is the living human being.

It is then imperative in the shaping of our lives that we think only those thoughts which are positive, and which build towards success and happiness. To think thoughts of fear, of self-doubt, of inability, or of defeat sets in motion the behavior that ultimately makes of us the embodiment of our negations.

It is negative thinking that results in getting little or nothing done in our lives. It is negative thinking that keeps us small in spite of the magnificent powers each one of us has to grow and excel and accomplish. It is also our negative thinking that dooms our loved ones, our wives and children, to cramped and unfulfilled lives because of their dependency upon us and our negations.

Our thoughts will make us small or big. The choice is ours.

HANG-OVER OF INFANCY

Just as there are drives that lead men to success, so also are there faults that cause men to fail.

Failure is performance below that of which we individually are capable. We can fail slightly, or we can fail abjectly. To what extent we do so depends largely on the kinds of personality and character faults that we possess. Some are more ruinous and destructive than others.

We may fail, for instance, because we are too self-centered; or because we are lazy, disloyal, dishonest, or undependable. It could be because we waste our time, are harassed by fears, have a lack of faith in ourselves, or are obsessed by greed. Or again it could be that we are conceited, or arrogant, indifferent to the interests of others, or negligent of the moral law.

Any personality or character fault is in a way a symptom of immaturity. It means that an improper relationship exists in some degree between us and the world of which we are a part. It means that we have not completely become adults. Some of the characteristics of infancy or of adolescence still are present in our relationship with ourselves and with others.

The single most dominant characteristic of the infant is self-centeredness. His relationship to others is entirely in terms of his own needs and desires. The characteristic of the adolescent is somewhat similar. It is a modified self-centeredness. He has become partially conscious of the needs and rights of those with whom he lives.

When a human being in his adult life remains excessively self-centered; when he continually shows a disregard for the interests of others, or an excessive concern about himself, we speak of him as being immature; that is, as being in essence an infant or an adolescent. There is a hang-over from infancy. It is perhaps the most serious of all the faults that cause men to fail. We speak of this fault as that of immaturity.

We expect and condone the self-centered activity of the infant because he is an infant, and it is his nature, in the interest of his survival, to act in this manner. We accept it with some reluctance from the adolescent because he is still part infant. But we abhor it in the adult who is expected to act like a mature man.

Immaturity is a perversion of nature's intent that an adult play the part of a man. This means that he must reach out toward others, and to seek the satisfaction of self in terms of the needs, and satisfactions, and well-being of the group. He is conscious of the whole of which he is a part. He is honest, just, dependable, fair, and trustworthy because his neighbor's welfare and good depend upon his being so. He does his share of the work because the group relies on his doing so. He stands on his own feet, handles his own problems, shares himself with those who need him.

To do otherwise is to act as an infant in an adult world. It means certain failure.

THE PRICELESS ASSET

Regardless of what other assets an individual may have, he cannot make full use of them in the shaping of his life unless he has the good will of the people with whom he associates.

Good will is the priceless intangible asset that is indispensable for individual well-being. We know statistically that from 80 to 90 per cent of those who fail in their jobs do so because they fall down on that aspect of their personal relationship which wins the good will of men toward them. We also know statistically that retail business establishments lose 66 out of every 100 customers every ten years purely and simply because they fail in the job of winning the good will of their customers.

Although we do not know statistically how many lives are spent below their normal potential because of the neglect of building up good will, we do know that it is almost impossible for an individual to fail who has behind him the force of the good will of the people with whom he lives and associates.

Good will can be defined with one word, namely, *belief.* Good will is a matter of others believing in us; believing in our mission; believing in our sincerity; believing in our honesty, our integrity, and our competence. It is belief that is created by our attitudes, our past performances, and by the ways we relate ourselves to others to make that relationship a satisfying experience for them.

Good will is the result of the external habits with which we relate ourselves to others, such as friendliness, dependability, honesty, tolerance, considerateness, helpfulness, and fair play.

To win the good will of others requires that we externally relate ourselves to them in ways that are pleasing to them and that help them make their daily lives more livable and satisfying. It is a matter af acting in an adult and grown-up fashion. It is speaking and acting as mature and emotionally healthy and well-balanced.

It is by what we do, more than by what we preach, that good will is won for us. It is our behavior that is the vital thing: our sincerity of purpose, our integrity, our friendliness, and our tactfulness. It is our willingness to take ourselves out of the center of attention and place the other person into it. It is our readiness to subordinate our own interests to the establishment and enlargement of those of others.

To win lasting good will we must have reverence for the personality of others. We must respect their dignity. We must show regard for their inalienable rights. We must be considerate of their feelings. We must be tolerant, understanding, willing and ready to give them the satisfactions they need for a richer life. In general, this means that good will is won by giving to others the same consideration we give to ourselves.

Yes, it is good will, which is no more nor less than having others believe in us, that is the priceless human asset.

THE SHAPER OF HIS DESTINY

Man can succeed only insofar as he lives in conformity with the fundamental laws of life.

He fails because he goes counter to one or more of these laws.

Man is not a puppet pulled here and there by the strings of fate.

He determines and shapes his own destiny.

He can be the creator of a successful life provided that he directs its course within the laws that operate in the physical, moral, and spiritual areas of the universe.

The certain effectiveness of these laws can be seen, for instance, in the physical realm in the unerring movement of the millions of stars and planets that make up our universe. One defection in the natural law that governs their movements would mean total destruction of all created things.

Man, too, operates in an orbit. It is regulated by certain physical, moral, and spiritual laws as certain and inexorable as those that govern the stars.

Let man step into space in a challenge to the law of gravitation, and its force pulls him against the earth to his destruction. Let him conform himself to this power of gravitation and he is safe. But let him disregard it and no power can help him avoid the consequences of his defiance of a law that is within the nature of things.

So it is in the moral and spiritual areas of his life. Let him live so his actions are needlessly harmful to his fellow men, and he goes contrary to the natural moral order. For life is so designed that the welfare of the part and the whole depends on man's cooperation and helpfulness to one another. He who acts otherwise is cast out by his own actions.

And in the spiritual realm of life, if a man does not believe in himself, in his innate dignity, and in his power to accomplish; if he does not believe in the goodness of his fellow man, or in a fundamental purpose of life, he cannot become what he is meant to be. The nature of his being is such that he cannot function effectively unless he has faith. It is a spiritual law of life.

Man is not, therefore, the victim of whimsical forces that conspire to make or break him, for the forces that assure fulfillment are known ones and are part of his nature. They are universal and eternal. He conforms or defies. If he fails, it is because he does not abide with these laws. It is he, not life, that is at fault.

IT'S A PUZZLEMENT

In speaking of life, the king in "The King and I" makes one of his expressive observations. He says, "It's a puzzlement."

There is little doubt that all of us more or less agree with him. This puzzlement is a universal experience. For instance, we don't know exactly what we do know. The things we are most certain of we really are not sure of. What we accept as fact today, may be proved tomorrow by science to be a fallacy. Our choicest beliefs are often the direct opposite of those held with equal intensity and sincerity by others. The unexpected and the seemingly illogical happen every day. The whole pattern of life becomes a crazy quilt to all of us at some time or other.

But it is not necessarily important that we understand the pattern of this great universe, or the infinite interworkings of the many forces that shape and determine human life. These are too great and complicated for our human minds. They belong in the province of God who designed and created them.

Our particular job is to see how we can fit ourselves into this picture, or how we can find and play our individual part in this great universal drama. What concerns us is how we can individually find direction, purpose, and security in this tremendous activity, the functioning of which we do not fully understand.

The task is really not as difficult as it may seem. What we need to do has been made obvious by the experiences of mankind. Wise men, too, have pointed out these obvious things to us. They could be summarized by saying that we must do what is in line with our own nature, and what is in harmony with natural and moral law. We believe what we must do could be stated in four simple precepts. They are:

1. Strictly adhere to the Ten Commandments.

2. Do our best each day.

3. Reach outward from ourselves into the service of others.

4. Fully trust the Divine Wisdom that designs and orders the scheme of things.

There is nothing particularly difficult about the doing of these. It is true that at first we must do them through conscious effort. We must force ourselves, as it were. But soon, as any other repeated acts, they become habitual—an automatic way of living. Their performance, like that of eating or walking, will no longer require special effort on our part. They become an integrated part of our personality.

Certainly the adoption of these four precepts as a way of life will make living a meaningful experience for us.

UPWARD THROUGH GROWING

We believe that most of us would like to go up to a level of working and living that is higher than the one we occupy at present. As the expression goes, we want "to go places."

We would like to get higher wages or earnings, to have better positions, to become socially more prominent, and to be more highly thought of and respected by our associates. In general, we would like to hold positions of greater prestige, income, and importance.

A mistake that many of us make, however, is that we expect someone else to catapult us into these positions. We want others to put us there; to push us upward to the desired loft. We want the force that elevates to be supplied, not by ourselves, but by someone outside of ourselves.

But that is not the way we "go places." Experience has shown that we get salary, and position, and stature by a process of personal growth. We "grow ourselves" into these things. Others may expose us to the opportunities to grow, but we ourselves do the growing which comes through a continuous process of conscious and deliberate self-development.

We grow by getting greater mastery of our jobs, by learning new skills, by acquiring better working habits, by improving our personalities, by extending the horizons of our minds, by increasing our self-sufficiency, and by assimilating the great thoughts, emotions, and ideals immortalized in our literature, art, philosophy, and religion.

Growth is not something that happens over night. It is a day-by-day continuous process. It is not something we can rush or hurry. It is an assimilative function that takes time. But what is of more importance in our understanding of it is the fact that it does not happen by itself. Nor can anyone else do it for us.

Each one of us, however, has opportunities unlimited to grow and, consequently, "to go places." A good place to start taking advantage of these opportunities is with our habit patterns. Each of us can reshape his habits of thinking, acting, working, and his habits of attitude into those that foster maturity and growth.

Our jobs, too, are media for the development of greater skills and know-how which foster growth. Our universities offer courses in practically every field of knowledge and culture. Our libraries are repositories of man's greatest thoughts and ideas. Our churches beckon us to the font of spiritual wisdom and understanding. All these are ways through which growth can be obtained if we will to take advantage of the opportunities they offer.

But first we must rid of ourselves of the fallacious idea of waiting for someone else to push us up into important places. The fact is that it is only through personal growth that we can rise to the heights above our present level. Once we make that thought the basis of our thinking, we have begun "to go places."

THE MARK OF OUR IMPRINT

To us as indviduals, the world is a confusingly large area of operation.

To relate ourselves to it in a meaningful way is a perplexing task. To find a purposive niche in it seems to many of us an impossible undertaking.

Our difficulty is that we look at the world en masse. By seeing it in terms of its complicated bigness, we put it beyond the reach of our touch. As a result, we can find no place to take hold in order to make ourselves a part of it. We can see no possible points of penetration for uniting ourselves with mankind's eternal quest to evolve to an ever higher self-fulfillment.

The question that occurs to many of us is, How can we as insignificant individuals take meaningful parts in this tremendous spectacle of activity, and leave the mark of our imprint upon it?

The answer to our question is simpler than we would suspect. It is to stop trying to relate ourselves in one embrace to the entire perplexing whole of life. It is, instead, to concentrate with all intensity on the relationships which are within the reach of our touch.

It is to aid, uplift, enlarge, or in any way better whatever falls within our reach, be it by direct relationships with those near to us as our loved ones in our homes, or by indirect relationships through group activities with those far away as the hungry or neglected children in far-distant lands.

Therefore, we need not search for places of possible integration with life. We need only to reach to what is within our touch. It is our neighbor who is the world of our concern. It is our loved ones, our fellow workers, our friends, the citizens of our immediate communities, and the human beings far and wide whom we can reach through group efforts. It is these who make up our individual worlds and who are the ones to whom we must relate ourselves if we would live our lives in a full and satisfying measure.

By placing our imprint on that which is directly or indirectly within our reach that we leave the mark of our imprint on the whole of the world and of life.

NOT ONE, BUT BOTH

It is generally agreed that the real substance of human relations lies in the heart of the individual. It is a matter of proper internal thoughts, feelings, and attitudes. Among these are those of justice, fair play, tolerance, selflessness, and compassion. If these are not present in the human heart, all external human relations are mere pretense. They are empty prattle.

In spite, however, of this essential basis of all genuine good human relations, the possession of the internal qualities or virtues is not by itself a guarantee of favorable relationships with our fellow men. Unfortunately, we can literally be saints and yet fail miserably in our relationships unless we have developed the external traits and habits of relating ourselves to others in terms of our virtues.

To influence others favorably, our virtues must be communicated to them. And it is for this reason that so much emphasis is placed in human relations on the external traits and habits of personality. It is through these external traits that we build the bridges between ourselves and our fellow human beings. It is through them that we relate ourselves to others. If this channel of communication is undeveloped or crude, our virtues remain relatively impotent as factors in bettering our relationships.

On the other hand, it is true that mere external habits of behavior do not lead to permanently good human relationships. Although they are the media of communication essential in the interrelationships of men, they do not create lasting good human relations unless they are outward expressions of corresponding internal thoughts, feelings, and attitudes.

External habits are modes of behavior that have become automatic because of repeated action. They can be good or bad. They can be developed in a sincere effort to make our relationships to others more pleasing and satisfying. Or, they can be developed as a false front to cover selfish ends. In this latter sense they are a low form of hypocrisy. The art and philosophy of good human relations will have no part in such behavior. It looks upon personality deceit of this kind as loathsome.

Inseparable in good human relations are the internal virtues which respect the rights and dignity of man, and the external traits with which the sincere and virtuous man relates himself to others in a pleasing and satisfying way. Without inner sincerity and virtue, relationships are shallow and often deceitful. Without the external habits, on the other hand, the sincere, good, and true within us will largely remain uncommunicated. In place of being the productive soil of satisfying human relationships, these will lie fallow within us.

It is, then, the proper internal thoughts, feeling, values, and attitudes outwardly expressed through habits of talking and acting that bring about permanently satisfying human relationships.

PUTTING IT INTO PRACTICE

We have been writing about some of the things that are believed to lead to success and happiness.

We have been discussing attitudes, work habits, drives and motives, fundamental moral principles, practices of good human relations, and many other things that experience has taught man to be fundamental to effective working and living.

There has been nothing new about most of these thoughts. As individuals, all of us have known them for the greater part of our lives. Mankind, on the other hand, has had knowledge of them for centuries. Some of them were taught to us by the great prophets of the race.

But, unfortunately, today, as throughout the years of the past, man has contented himself too much with the possession of the mere knowledge of these principles of good living. Man frequently has not made them an integral part of his life. He has given lip service to them but has not fully put them into practice.

This has been true of the Ten Commandments of Moses. It has been true of the beautiful and wise principles taught us by Christ. It is equally true of the everyday bits of knowledge and wisdom that come to us as the result of observation and experience.

Yet, unfortuantely, as we all know, knowledge of the moral law, for instance, does not by itself make us virtuous. Knowledge of the factors that lead to success and happiness does not by itself bring that success or happiness.

Knowledge of ways of making our lives effective does not by itself bring effectiveness. Knowledge of the ways and means to good human relationship does not by itself further these relationships. It is only by putting into practice the knowledge we have that we can gain the ends or purposes desired. We become virtuous only by being honest, truthful, and just. We become successful in our jobs only by doing that which makes for success. We become proficient in human relations only by actually being friendly, helpful, considerate, and understanding.

A salesman becomes successful only if he presents his proposition effectively to a sufficiently large number of people each day. An executive becomes effective insofar as he does the things that make him a leader of his people. A man becomes a man only when he acts maturely in his relationship to himself and to others. It is not a store of knowledge of right principles that gives him stature and effectiveness. It is rather the actual application of these principles in his every activity. In short, it is practicing what he knows and what he preaches.

ABSOLUTE ASSURANCE THROUGH FAITH

---◈---

Faith in the greatness and wisdom of God is by far the most important factor in giving direction, purpose, and security to our lives.

We do not mean blind faith, but rather one that has its roots in our daily experiences of observing the workings of divine wisdom in the greatness of God's works. We mean faith that has grown strong and impregnable because we have seen the sun, and the moon, and the stars guided unerringly in their courses.

We mean faith that grew because we saw the seed spring into the living flower; because we witnessed year after year, the sap rising into the trees, the awakening of the buds, the coming of the leaves, the ripening of the fruit, and then the receding of the sap for the long winter's sleep.

We mean faith that comes to us as we watch the bird wing its way in the unmarked skies, faith that comes to us as we touch the soft, green blade of grass, or as we behold the infant that evolved from the microscopic seed placed in the womb of its mother.

It is this faith in the God who designs, and integrates, and guides all these tremendous forces into one universal unit, that takes away from life its "puzzlement" and gives real direction and purpose to it.

How can man behold all of the innumerable manifestations of greatness, and wisdom, and purpose in the universe, and yet fail to see meaning and direction in his own life? Since God directs wisely the movements of the planets, the stars, the trees, the birds, and of the involuntary physical processes of life, such as the unfolding of the ovum into the man, does he not also direct wisely the life of man?

If there is purpose and direction in all other aspects of the universe, is it not so also in man's life, around which all things center and toward which all things are directed? It is this belief in the greatness and wisdom of God, and the trust in His purposes and in His ways that give man absolute assurance that there is a purpose and direction in his life, and that he is meant to play a specific part in the fulfillment of an eternal plan.

There is no room for "puzzlement" if he trusts, and this is particularly true when the basis of his trust is, as we have seen, incontestable in the light of his own everyday observations and experiences.

Man needs but to remember constantly that which was so beautifully stated by Robert Browning in his "Pippa Passes,"

> God's in His heaven
> All's right with the world.

GETTING ALONG WITH PEOPLE

Industrial psychologists and personnel men are convinced that good personality is by far the most important factor in success on a job.

They consider job knowledge or skill as fundamental, and, of course, required. But on the basis of countless case histories, they believe it to be less than a 20% factor in success or failure.

They believe the determining item to be an 80% to 90% superstructure of personality traits that cause people to respond favorably or unfavorably to us.

Good personality is made up of traits and habits that help us get along well with others. It is, then, the habits of getting along with people that count most.

It is the things we do that win the friendship, respect, confidence, and loyalty of others that ultimately determine our success.

It is the habits of sympathy and understanding, of friendliness and helpfulness, of sincerity and dependability.

It is the getting our thinking off ourselves, and concentrating it on the other fellow. It is showing him, through our attitude and our actions, that his interests and needs come first.

It is actually placing his well-being uppermost in our minds and hearts and daily actions.

HOLDING FAST TO BASIC VALUES

To hold fast to our sense of basic values is our most urgent need today.

We are living in an era in which the emphasis on technological and scientific developments has brought to us a near mastery of the material forces of nature. This mastery, however, promises a revolution in our way of living. Many of our traditional concepts of man's relationship to the physical world are being totally obliterated. Seemingly incalculable and unconquerable forces of his environment, such as atomic energy, supersonic speed, and outer space, are rapidly being mastered by him. Even the diseases that in the past decimated the human race are now with three or four exceptions harmless in the wake of his medical discoveries.

All of these things are good, for they help man to make a better and longer life for himself and his fellow men. That is to say, they are good if he uses them constructively to make a better world for the races of men. They are equally bad and dangerous, however, if in the hands of the unjust and unscrupulous they are used destructively for selfish aggrandizement.

Atomic energy, conquest of outer space, and supersonic speed can be used by men and nations of ill will and moral depravity to enslave, even to blast from the face of the earth, those who do not subscribe to the will of the powerful.

How man will use his new mastery depends wholly on one thing. It is on, What values he will accept as a way of life. If he continues to hold fast to the basic values of living taught to him by experience, and clarified for him by the wise men and teachers of the past, man can look forward to a future of unprecedented well-being.

And never have the basic values of life been more clearly and succinctly given to us than by Christ. Perhaps all of us could profit greatly for ourselves and our progeny by reviewing again and again the basic values as He taught them.

Over and over again He spoke of integrity, of justice, and of love for one another. He spoke of the dignity of the individual human being, and of the brotherhood of man. He spoke of truthfulness, of mercy, and of mutual understanding. He never ceased to speak of man's responsibility to love his fellow man, and of his obligation to be his brother's keeper. He summarized the entire body of his teachings by two simple commands: "Love thy God above all things, and love thy neighbor as thyself."

These are the values men of integrity, good will, and social responsibility accept as the basic values of life. And, they are man's only certain safeguard today of future survival, regardless from what source of authority he accepts their validity.

If man holds fast to these basic values his newly found mastery of the forces of nature will elevate the lives of all mankind. If, on the other hand, he discards them as antiquated, or replaces them with purely selfish and technological values, the future of mankind is necessarily a foreboding one.

A deepened sense of basic values is for us individually and collectively our only guarantee for the future.

CPSIA information can be obtained
at www.ICGtesting.com
Printed in the USA
LVHW081317190520
656058LV00013B/141

9 781258 284800